EDUCATION REPORT CARD Schools on the Line

D0628041

Timely Reports to Keep
Journalists, Scholars and the Public
Abreast of Developing Issues, Events and Trends

Editorial Research Reports
Published by Congressional Quarterly Inc.
1414 22nd Street, N.W.
Washington, D.C. 20037

About the Cover

The cover was designed by Assistant Art Director Robert Redding

PRINTED IN THE UNITED STATES OF AMERICA

Editor, Hoyt Gimlin
Associate Editor, Martha V. Gottron
Editorial Assistants, Leah Klumph, Elizabeth Furbush
Production Manager, I. D. Fuller
Assistant Production Manager, Maceo Mayo

Library of Congress Cataloging in Publication Data

Main entry under title:

Education report card.

Reports originally published in Editorial research reports.
Bibliography: p.
Includes index.
1. Education — United States — 1965-   . 2. Public schools — United States.   I. Congressional Quarterly, inc.
II. Editorial research reports.
LA217.E3664   1985   370´.973   84-19932
ISBN 0-87187-338-9

Contents

Foreword

"Our society and its educational institutions seem to have lost sight of the basic purposes of schooling, and of the high expectations and disciplined effort needed to attain them," the National Commission on Education in Excellence wrote in April 1983. "If an unfriendly foreign power had attempted to impose on America the mediocre educational performance that exists today, we might well have viewed it as an act of war. As it stands, we have allowed this to happen to ourselves. We have even squandered the gains in student achievement made in the wake of the Sputnik challenge."

The commission's warnings fell on receptive ears. The response to its recommendations and those of several other studies released in succeeding months has been fulsome. Every state has either enacted or is considering some sort of educational reform, from lengthening the school day to raising graduation requirements, even to raising taxes to pay for improvements. Above all else, the reformers eye the teachers, insisting that schools can make a difference provided administrators and teachers set high academic standards and expect the students to perform.

This puts teachers at the storm center of the movement. While some say merit pay is the best way to attract talented teachers, others say base salaries should be increased to compete with industry. Either way, school systems must raise additional money to finance their educational reforms. But obviously money isn't everything. Family and society pressures on youths can also interfere with the education process. And what of the children our education system has already failed? According to various estimates, 13 percent of all 17-year-olds are functionally illiterate; as many as 850,000 pupils drop out of school every year.

The question of what role religion should play in the nation's public schools is very much with us. It is an emotional issue, especially prominent in this presidential election year, pitting fervently held beliefs and values against each other. The struggle to resolve it could obscure other equally important educational issues.

Reports in this volume examine the directions educational reform is taking in elementary and secondary schools, in colleges and universities and in the teaching profession. Other Reports look at the controversies surrounding school prayer and textbook content, while still others examine illiteracy and the pressures on youth. These are among the many factors that shape the education of the nation's children and so its future.

Martha V. Gottron
Associate Editor

September 1984
Washington, D.C.

STATUS
OF THE
SCHOOLS

by

Roger Thompson

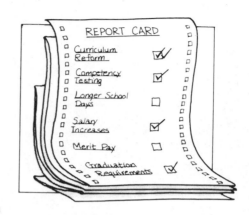

Aug. 24
1 9 8 4

STATUS OF THE SCHOOLS

THE CRISIS in America's classrooms that has grabbed head-lines for more than a year may not be over, but massive help is on the way. Ever since April 1983, when a federal commission warned the nation of a "rising tide of mediocrity" in its schools, educators, legislators and the public in general have debated how to improve the quality of education in America. More than that, the federal government and most states have taken steps to upgrade education in the nation's public schools. "There has been in the last 12 months more concerted nationwide action than at any other time in my memory and that includes [the activity following the 1957 Soviet launch of] Sputnik," said Ernest L. Boyer, president of the Carnegie Foundation for the Advancement of Learning.[1]

Every state has either already enacted or is considering in-stituting reforms that affect all facets of the educational system, from upgrading school curricula and raising high school gradua-tion requirements to lengthening the school day and year to raising teachers' salaries, rewarding quality teaching and stiffening teacher certification requirements. "The national education reform movement is of epical proportions," said Mil-ton Goldberg, who served as executive director of the National Commission on Excellence in Education.[2] "One of the things that we are most pleased about," Goldberg added, "is that it is not just educators who are participating. It is political leaders, business and industry, and citizens."

It was the National Commission on Excellence in Education that triggered the upsurge in attention to public education with publication on April 26, 1983, of "A Nation At Risk: The Imper-ative for Educational Reform." [3] It warned in blunt language that "the educational foundations of our society are presently being eroded by a rising tide of mediocrity that threatens our very future as a nation and a people." In succeeding months another half dozen independent studies buttressed the commis-

---

[1] Quoted in *The New York Times*, Aug. 5, 1984.
[2] Goldberg and other persons quoted in this report were interviewed by the author unless otherwise indicated.
[3] The 18-member commission, composed primarily of educators, was appointed by Education Secretary T. H. Bell on Aug. 26, 1981, to assess the quality of education at all levels in both public and private schools. The commission disbanded in August 1983.

sion's findings.[4] While they differed in specific recommendations for change, these reports shared a sense of urgency about the need to improve public education.

The activity of the last year has revived Americans' confidence in the public schools, according to a Gallup Poll released Aug. 5. The poll, conducted in May, found that 42 percent of American adults give an A or B grade to their local public schools, up more than a third over the previous year when 31 percent of the respondents gave the schools similar marks. Gallup also reported an increased willingness among those interviewed to pay for their children's education. The poll found 41 percent would vote for higher taxes to support their local schools, only two points higher than the previous year but an 11-point gain since a similar poll was conducted in 1981.[5] However, 47 percent continue to oppose tax increases for the schools. Another important sign of renewed public interest in the schools is a surge in National Parent Teacher Association (PTA) membership, which increased by 70,000 last year after a 20-year decline.[6]

Mary Hatwood Futrell, president of the National Education Association, the nation's largest teachers' organization, said the Gallup findings "stand as convincing evidence that all the attention lavished on education over the past 18 months has had a healthy effect." Gary L. Bauer, deputy under secretary of education, said, "No one believes the crisis is over, but as you travel around the country you get the sense that we have turned the corner on educational reform." [7]

Taking Stock of Recent Developments

Efforts to improve the quality of education are not new; earlier post-World War II education movements focused primarily on teaching styles or course content. The striking characteristic of the ongoing drive is that it encompasses nearly every aspect of schooling, from what is taught to how teachers are trained. The variety of issues under review helps explain the broad-based participation of educators, state and local officials, business leaders and citizens in charting the course of change. And it is this widespread support that has helped make it

---

[4] Task Force on Education for Economic Growth, "Action for Excellence: A Comprehensive Plan to Improve Our Nation's Schools," Education Commission of the States, June 1983; The National Science Board, "Educating Americans for the 21st Century," 1983; The Twentieth Century Fund Task Force on Federal Elementary and Secondary Education Policy, "Making the Grade," 1983; John I. Goodlad, *A Place Called School: Prospects for the Future,* McGraw-Hill, 1983; Ernest L. Boyer, *High School, A Report on Secondary Education in America,* Harper and Row, 1983; Theodore R. Sizer, *Horace's Compromise — The Dilemma of the American High School,* Houghton Mifflin, 1984.

[5] The Gallup Poll results will be published in the September issue of *Phi Delta Kappan* magazine.

[6] Department of Education, "The Nation Responds, Recent Efforts to Improve Education," May 1984, p. 12.

[7] Futrell and Bauer were quoted in *The New York Times,* Aug. 5, 1984.

possible for the states to adopt so many reform initiatives in such a short period.

According to a survey issued in May by the Department of Education, 35 states have tightened high school graduation requirements, 22 have revised the curriculum, 15 have extended the school day and/or school year; 14 have raised teachers' salaries and six have adopted plans to reward exceptional teachers *(see p. 7)*. Many of these and other actions are under consideration in all of the other states.[8] A second survey of recent activity, this one by the Education Commission of the States, also found that 15 states have passed or are considering tax increases for education and that 45 states now have businesses involved in helping public schools.[9]

Several states have adopted particularly tough or innovative reforms. Florida in July 1983 increased its high school graduation requirements to 24 academic credits — highest in the nation — effective in 1986-87 and enacted a merit-pay plan for teachers. California the same month established a mentor teacher program paying an annual bonus of at least $4,000 to those chosen to guide beginning teachers, increased beginning teacher salaries to $18,000 a year, raised graduation requirements and lengthened the school day and year. Arkansas in November 1983 raised its sales tax 1 cent to pay for $154 million in school improvements, including higher teacher salaries, a

---

[8] Department of Education, *op. cit.*

[9] Task Force on Education for Economic Growth, "Action in the States," Education Commission of the States, July 1984. The Education Commission of the States is a non-profit organization based in Denver. It conducts education policy research on behalf of public officials and educators in its 48 member states.

longer school day and year, stricter graduation requirements and tougher grade promotion policies.[10]

Business Involvement in Public Schools

Not all the money for new programs is coming from state legislatures. Private foundations, which have traditionally channeled most of their education dollars into colleges, are showing a greater interest in elementary and secondary schools. A number of foundations are providing "venture capital" to help schools test some of the ideas recommended by last year's flurry of reports. One such program is managed by the National Association of Secondary School Principals, with funding from the Atlantic Richfield Foundation. Competitive grants of up to $50,000 will be awarded to 25 high schools implementing recommendations of *High School*, a report sponsored by the Carnegie Foundation for the Advancement of Teaching.

The Ford Foundation in 1982 and 1983 awarded $1,000 to each of 202 urban high schools that had improved significantly over the past decade. One hundred of those schools received a second award of $20,000 each to further their efforts.[11] The West Virginia Education Foundation plans a statewide program that will award $300 grants to innovative teachers and $2,500 grants to superintendents.

Existing business partnerships with schools are expanding and new programs are starting in record numbers. Some companies have established flexitime or released-time policies that allow employees to do volunteer work in schools. Others are offering teachers summer employment or participating in student job-training programs. The American Council on Life Insurance in cooperation with the St. Louis public schools has developed a how-to kit on business-school collaboration for its 600 member companies.

Some business-school efforts are statewide in scope. The California Roundtable, composed of executive officers of 88 of the states's major businesses, helped rally political support for the educational measures approved by the California Legislature in 1983. The Minnesota Business Partnership, joined by executive officers from 68 of the state's key businesses, has conducted a yearlong study of the state's public schools and is drafting policy recommendations to hand the state Legislature this fall.

Other efforts are confined to individual school districts. In

---

[10] For background on merit pay and career ladders, see "Teachers: The Push for Excellence," *E.R.R.*, 1984 Vol I., pp. 291-306.

[11] The foundation has published a 106-page report entitled "City High Schools: A Recognition of Progress," to encourage other schools to launch improvement programs.

Actions to Improve Education

The following table shows which states have recently enacted (✔) or are considering (●) reforms in six specific areas. Many states have also taken a number of other actions to improve the quality of education including competency testing for students, improved discipline, tougher teacher training and certification programs and development programs for school administrators.

	Curriculum Reform	Graduation Requirements	Longer School Day	Longer School Year	Salary Increases	Career Ladders
Ala.	✔	✔			●	
Alaska	✔	●				
Ariz.	✔	✔		●	●	●
Ark.	✔	✔	✔	✔	✔	
Calif.	✔	✔		✔	✔	✔
Colo.	●	●		●		●
Conn.		●			●	●
Del.	●	✔	●		✔	●
D.C.	✔	✔	✔		✔	●
Fla.	●	✔	✔	✔	✔	✔
Ga.		✔	●	●	✔	
Hawaii	●			●	●	✔
Idaho	●	✔	✔		✔	✔
Ill.	●	✔	●		●	✔
Ind.	✔	✔				
Iowa	✔					
Kan.	●	✔			●	●
Ky.	✔	✔			●	●
La.	✔	✔	✔		●	
Maine		●			●	●
Md.	●	●				●
Mass.	●			●	●	●
Mich.	✔	✔	✔	✔	✔	
Minn.	●	●				●
Miss.	●	●	●	●	✔	●
Mo.		✔	●			●
Mont.	✔	✔				

	Curriculum Reform	Graduation Requirements	Longer School Day	Longer School Year	Salary Increases	Career Ladders
Neb.	●	●	●	●	●	
Nev.	●	✔			●	●
N.H.	●	●				
N.J.	●	✔			●	●
N.M.	✔	✔				●
N.Y.	✔	✔		✔	●	●
N.C.	●	✔	✔	✔	●	●
N.D.		✔	✔			
Ohio	●	✔	●	●	✔	●
Okla.		✔				
Ore.	●	✔	●	●		●
Pa.	✔	✔				●
R.I.	●	●				
S.C.	●	●	●	●	●	
S.D.	●	✔				
Tenn.	✔	✔		✔	✔	✔
Texas	✔	✔		●	●	●
Utah	●	✔	●			✔
Vt.	✔	✔	●	●		●
Va.	✔	✔			✔	●
Wash.	✔	✔			●	●
W.Va.	✔	●			✔	●
Wis.	✔	✔	●	●	●	●
Wyo.	●	●				
✔ Total	22	35	8	7	14	6
● Total	23	13	13	14	20	24
Total	45	48	21	21	34	30

Source: Department of Education, "The Nation Responds," May 1984.

Dallas, over 1,000 businesses have "adopted" nearly all of the city's more than 200 public schools. Coordinated by the local Chamber of Commerce, business sponsors provide volunteer tutors and donate funds, equipment and materials to their adopted schools. Los Angeles and Memphis city schools also have extensive adopt-a-school programs. The Philadelphia Alliance for Teaching Humanities in the Schools is a business-public school partnership whose goal is to improve high school writing instruction. The group expects to raise $2.3 million for the project over the next three years.

Words of Caution About Current Reforms

"We've made progress, but if we stop here, we'll quickly find ourselves falling behind again," said Delaware Gov. Pierre S. DuPont IV, chairman of the Task Force on Education for Economic Growth. There are some, however, who question whether all the apparent progress is real. Susan J. Rosenholtz, an assistant professor of education at Vanderbilt University in Nashville, Tenn., warns that some reform ideas run counter to established education research findings.[12]

Research indicates, for example, that many academically talented college students choose not to become teachers because beginning salaries are well below those offered in private-sector jobs, Rosenholtz writes. The average starting salary for teachers in 1981-82 was $12,769, compared with $15,444 for liberal arts majors and $20,364 for computer science majors.[13] However, the performance-based pay plans that some states have adopted and others are considering would do little to address this issue because they require new teachers to wait for years to qualify for pay bonuses, Rosenholtz says. Therefore, higher base salaries, not pay incentives, would be a more effective way to attract top students into teaching, she concludes.

John A. Thompson of the University of Hawaii Department of Educational Administration reminds educators to consider the costs of performance-pay plans. Thompson calculated the cost of typical merit-pay and career-ladder plans at roughly $127 and $162 per pupil each year. While that may not be prohibitive, it is expensive, he said.[14] At least one group questions what schools will get in return for the money spent. "The information available from past research ... provides little convincing evidence — one way or the other — on whether teacher merit pay plans ... have substantially affected student achievement, teacher retention rates, or the ability to attract

---

[12] Susan J. Rosenholtz, "Political Myths About Reforming the Teaching Profession," Working Paper No. 4, Education Commission of the States, July 1984.
[13] "The American Teacher," Feistritzer Publications, 1983.
[14] John A. Thompson, "Cost Factors of Paying Teachers for Performance," Working Paper No. 4, Education Commission of the States, May 1984.

new quality teachers," the authors of an Urban Institute report wrote in January 1984.[15]

Spending more to extend the school day or lengthen the school year also may not produce the desired increase in learning, says Allan Odden, director of the Education Finance Center of the Education Commission of the States. He calculates that lengthening the typical school day from 6.5 hours to 8 hours would cost more than $20 billion nationwide; lengthening the school year from 180 days to 220 days would cost another $20 billion. "There is little support from research to justify such large expenditures to increase school time, even though the arguments in favor of this strategy seem valid on the surface," Odden says.[16]

Course of Change

EDUCATIONAL THEORIES have come and gone in successive waves since World War II. The nation's first educational "crisis" in the postwar era emerged in the early 1950s in reaction to the tenets of progressive education. The progressive movement took root around the turn of the century as educators sought to turn the schools away from the narrow formalism of the 19th century to broader tasks associated with a rapidly changing industrial society.[17] It made children, not subject matter, the focus of concern. The schools began to place more emphasis on the social and emotional development of students and less on such traditional academic subjects as mathematics, literature, history and languages. School curricula were expanded to include non-academic courses on health and the family.

After the war, critics of progressive education charged that it fostered poor classroom discipline, de-emphasized mastery of basic subject matter, abandoned the study of Western culture and failed to teach respect for hard, sustained work. Influential books, such as Arthur Bestor's *Educational Wastelands* (1953) and Albert Lynd's *Quackery in the Public Schools* (1953), took educators to task for abandoning rigorous intellectual training. Others found fault with teaching methods. Rudolf Flesch started a national debate in 1955 with publication of *Why*

[15] Harry P. Hatry and John M. Greiner, "Issues in Teacher Incentive Plans," The Urban Institute, Washington, D.C., January 1984.
[16] Allan Odden, "Financing Educational Excellence," *Phi Delta Kappan*, January 1984, p. 315.
[17] For background, see "Education's Return to Basics," *E.R.R.*, 1975 Vol. II, pp. 667-682.

Johnny Can't Read, an attack on the "look-say" method of reading instruction, which teaches children to recognize hundreds of words by sight before teaching them the mechanics of phonics. Flesch maintained that the only way to make children independent readers was through a "phonics first" approach.[18]

By the time the Soviets launched the first Earth satellite in October 1957, the nation was primed for change. Sputnik became a symbol of the cost of indifference to educational excellence. Broad public support for a federal response to the Soviet challenge led Congress to pass the National Defense Education Act of 1958 to encourage college students to study science, mathematics and foreign languages.

At the local level, James B. Conant's *American High School Today* (1959) provided a blueprint for secondary-school reorganization. Conant, a former Harvard University president, urged consolidation of small secondary schools into "comprehensive high schools" that would challenge college-bound students with advanced course work while providing solid general and vocational instruction to other students. His book revived interest in academic rigor and led to a wave of high school consolidations across the country. Concurrently, study groups at various universities developed and marketed new math and science textbooks designed to attract more students into scientific study.

By the end of the 1960s, critics again were declaring an educational crisis. Charles E. Silberman's best-seller *Crisis in the Classroom* (1970) popularized the notion that the pendulum had swung too far toward academic rigor at the expense of those being taught. Silberman and others held that schools rewarded students for being docile and obedient, not for thinking and acting independently. They believed that every child should experience school for its own sake and not merely as a preparation for something later on in life. With the English primary schools' open, informal style as a model, "open classrooms" quickly spread. "Relevance" gained popularity as a rationale for curriculum design. High schools and colleges lowered academic course requirements and substituted new offerings designed to appeal to student interests.

By the mid-1970s this educational experimentation was viewed with widespread disfavor. Once again critics said that schools had become too lax in teaching basic reading, writing and math skills. News stories told of high school graduates who could not read or make change and reported a steady decline in

---

[18] In *Why Johnny Still Can't Read* (1981), Flesch said 85 percent of all schools still used the look-say method despite convincing evidence favoring the phonics approach. For background see "Illiteracy in America," *E.R.R.*, 1983 Vol. I, pp. 475-490.

Outlook for Private Schools

Enrollment in private schools has dropped in the last few years, but not as much as in the public schools. Between 1970 and 1982, total private school enrollment fell from 5.4 million to 5.1 million, a 5 percent decline compared with the 14 percent drop experienced by the public schools.

The loss of about two million Catholic-school students in little more than a decade was largely offset by rises in other private schools. Most non-Catholic private schools reported enrollment increases of 2-10 percent in 1982-83, the last year for which figures are available. Catholic schools, which enroll approximately 60 percent of all private school students, reported a decline of about 2 percent for the past two years.

Private school enrollment is projected to increase slightly to 5.3 million by 1992, accounting for 11 percent of the total enrollment in elementary and secondary schools. That represents no change from 1982 and only a slight increase from the 10.5 percent registered in 1970, according to the National Center for Education Statistics.

Tuition tax credits for parents who choose private education for their children have been at the top of the private schools' legislative agenda for more than a decade. Congress has consistently rebuffed attempts to pass such a measure, but supporters of the idea say a Supreme Court ruling last fall may help them achieve their goals at the state level.

The court in *Mueller v. Allen* (1983) upheld a Minnesota law that permits parents to claim state income tax deductions of up to $700 for educational expenses including tuition, transportation, non-religious textbooks, supplies and fees. The court upheld the law chiefly because it offers the deductions to both public- and private-school parents, although in practice benefits accrue primarily to private-school parents.

The court's ruling shifted the tuition-tax-credit battle to state legislatures this year, where lawmakers in 13 states told *Education Week* last spring they had introduced or planned to introduce legislation modeled after the Minnesota law. However, by mid-August, none of the 13 had passed Minnesota-style tax credits, according to the Education Commission of the States.

---

high school seniors' scores on college entrance exams. Curricula began to emphasize basic academic instruction again and many states imposed higher standards on the schools by requiring students to pass competency tests for grade promotion and/or graduation.[19]

---

[19] A July 1984 survey by the Education Commission of the States found that 19 states require minimum reading and math skills for high school graduation, 21 test for remediation at various grade levels and five test for grade promotion. Twenty-eight states have enacted at least one of these requirements. For background, see "Competency Tests," *E.R.R.*, 1978 Vol. II, pp. 603-618.

The ongoing "back-to-basics" movement is accompanied by a drive to improve the quality of the nation's public school teachers. In addition to salary raises and merit pay plans to recruit and retain talented teachers, 25 states have enacted laws requiring prospective teachers to pass proficiency tests before receiving certification. More recently, 17 states have acted to require college students to pass proficiency tests to enter teacher training.[20]

Quest for Equal Educational Opportunity

Often overshadowing the debate on instruction was the struggle to provide equal educational opportunity to the nation's minorities, women, the handicapped and bilingual children. The U.S. Supreme Court outlawed state-mandated "separate but equal" public schools in its famous *Brown v. Board of Education* decision of May 17, 1954. But the court left it to lower courts and the states to implement desegregation, and the pace was slow. By 1964 less than 2 percent of black pupils in the former Confederate states were attending desegregated schools. Congress sought to speed desegregation with passage of the Civil Rights Act of 1964, which made technical and financial assistance available to desegregating school districts and, for the first time, allowed the federal government to withhold funds from any school district practicing discrimination.

Many school districts, however, continued to find ways to resist desegregation. It was not until 1971, in *Swann v. Charlotte-Mecklenburg County Board of Education*, that the Supreme Court upheld busing as a valid means to achieve desegregation. In that same case the court also held that certain actions previously justified as *de facto* segregation — the kind that results from housing patterns — might actually be deliberate or *de jure* segregation and therefore subject to court intervention. As a result, segregated school systems in Northern states came under court scrutiny; Denver, Boston, San Francisco, Indianapolis, Wilmington, Del., and Omaha, Neb., were among those cities where courts found officially sanctioned segregation.

Conversely, the Supreme Court has ruled that genuine *de facto* segregation is not a violation of the Constitution. This sort of segregation affects most metropolitan areas where predominantly black central-city schools are ringed by largely white suburban school districts. In a landmark 1974 case involving the Detroit city schools, *Milliken v. Bradley*, the high court overturned a lower court order to bus students among 54 school districts in three counties to desegregate the city schools. The

---

[20] For background, see "Teachers: The Push for Excellence," *E.R.R.*, 1984 Vol. I, pp. 291-306.

majority held that a multi-district remedy was not appropriate unless all of the districts involved were found responsible for the segregation to be remedied.[21] Desegregation efforts have had mixed success. The number of blacks in the South attending predominantly black schools dropped from 81 percent in 1968 to 57 percent in 1980.[22] By contrast, schools in the Northeast grew more segregated during the same period. Blacks attending predominantly black public schools increased from 67 percent to 80 percent.

Busing as a desegregation tool has never been popular, and at least one city is abandoning it. In Norfork, Va., a U.S. District Court judge has upheld the school board's plan to halt busing for the district's 20,000 elementary-school students and again allow children to attend classes in neighborhood schools. The board put off implementing its plan a year, until the fall of 1985, to develop "greater confidence among Norfork's black leadership that it's a sound plan," said board chairman Thomas G. Johnson Jr.[23] Seventeen of the districts's 35 elementary schools would be predominantly black under the neighborhood plan. The plan is being appealed to the 4th U.S. Circuit Court of Appeals in Richmond. Black leaders fear it will mean a return to the "separate-but-equal" doctrine outlawed by the Supreme Court 30 years ago.

Growth of Federal Education Programs

Passage of the Civil Rights Act of 1964 cleared the way for congressional approval a year later of the first federal general aid bill for public education. By barring federal aid to segregated schools, the 1964 civil rights law ended the longstanding controversy over federal support for the South's dual school system. The remaining objection to federal aid was fear that federal money would bring federal control of local schools. Congress broke this impasse by directing federal aid to the nation's disadvantaged children. The key provision of the Elementary and Secondary Education Act, signed by President Johnson on

[21] For background, see "Busing Reappraisal," *E.R.R.*, 1975 Vol. II, pp. 947-962.; and "Desegregation After 20 Years," *E.R.R.*, 1974 Vol. I, pp. 325-341.
[22] Figures from Gary Orfield, "Public School Desegregation in the United States between 1968-1980," Joint Center for Political Studies, Washington, D.C.
[23] Quoted in *The Washington Post*, July 24, 1984.

April 11, 1965, was Title 1, which made grants to schools to help them offset the negative effects of poverty on student achievement. The cost of this compensatory education program has grown from slightly more than $1 billion in fiscal 1966 to $3.5 billion in fiscal 1984.

In the early 1970s, Congress significantly expanded educational opportunities for women and handicapped children. In 1972 Congress barred discrimination in schools on the basis of sex. To enforce that ban the federal government could withhold federal education aid to any school that discriminated against women in admissions, classes, employment and financial aid. The most visible impact at all levels of school has been in athletic programs for women; the 1972 law required that schools sponsoring interscholastic or intramural sports must provide equal athletic opportunity for members of both sexes, including establishing women's teams, and giving them coaches and adequate training and playing facilities.[24]

In 1975, Congress passed the Education for All Handicapped Children Act, which required states to provide free, adequate education for handicapped pupils by Sept. 1, 1980, and authorized grants to help the states meet the added expenses associated with educating the handicapped. Federal funds for this effort amounted to $1.2 billion in fiscal year 1984.[25]

The federal government expanded its bilingual education program following a 1974 Supreme Court decision that required schools to provide special aid to children who did not speak English. Failure to do so, the court said in *Lau v. Nichols*, would be a violation of the Civil Rights Act of 1964, which banned discrimination on the basis of national origin. Federal aid generally goes only to those schools that give children instruction in their native languages in academic subjects while they are learning English.

The Carter administration caused an uproar in late 1980 when it proposed new regulations that would have required any school receiving federal funding for any purpose to teach non-English-speaking students in their native language until they had mastered English. Congress, under pressure from outraged school officials, postponed enforcement of the regulations, and the Reagan administration revoked them. The administration,

[24] There is some fear that a recent Supreme Court ruling may have undercut the impact of the 1972 law, In *Grove City College v. Bell*, the court narrowly interpreted Title IX of the Education Amendments of 1972 to hold that the ban on discrimination applied only to those programs receiving federal aid. Legislation declaring that the discrimination ban applies to an entire institution if any part of it receives federal aid is pending in Congress. For background, see "Women in Sports," *E.R.R.*, 1977 Vol I., pp. 331-346.
[25] For background, see "Mainstreaming: Handicapped Children in the Classroom," *E.R.R.*, 1981 Vol. II, pp. 535-548.

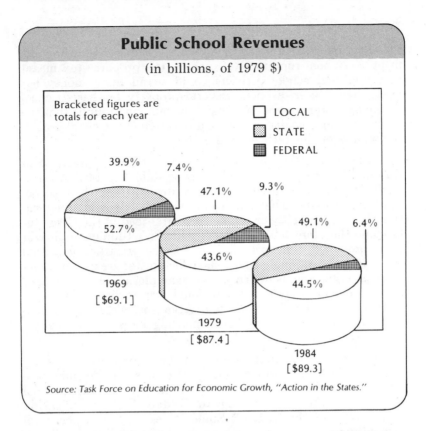

Public School Revenues

(in billions, of 1979 $)

Bracketed figures are totals for each year

☐ LOCAL
▨ STATE
▦ FEDERAL

39.9%   7.4%
47.1%   9.3%
52.7%
43.6%   49.1%   6.4%
44.5%

1969
[$69.1]

1979
[$87.4]

1984
[$89.3]

Source: Task Force on Education for Economic Growth, "Action in the States."

however, generated another controversy by recommending that federal aid be granted to bilingual programs that do not include instruction in the children's mother tongue.[26]

Dominant State Role in School Financing

Despite the loud controversies that often surround them, federal elementary and secondary education aid programs account for a relatively small portion of the overall school budget. Federal expenditures as a percentage of all education spending reached a peak of 9 percent in 1979-80 and have declined since to an estimated 6.4 percent in 1983-84, due largely to cuts in the aid programs. Federal spending for education programs in fiscal 1984 was nearly $7 billion. However, while federal aid may make up only a small portion of any school's budget, its proponents are quick to point out that much of it is earmarked for students and activities traditionally under-funded at the state and local levels.

Since the late 1960s, significant changes in public school financing have taken place at the state and local levels, where lawsuits over equity have lessened dependency on property

[26] For background, see *Congressional Quarterly Weekly Report*, April 7, 1984, p. 811.

taxes and led states for the first time to assume the leading role in public school funding. Reliance on the property tax meant that wealthier school districts could spend more money per pupil than poorer districts. Several property tax-based school financing systems were challenged in court on grounds that the variations between districts were a violation of the equal protection clause of the 14th Amendment.

However, in 1973 the Supreme Court, in *Rodriguez v. San Antonio Independent School District*, said the 14th Amendment could not be used to force states to alter their school financing systems. The court found that the right to an education was not explicitly or implicitly guaranteed in the Constitution and therefore could not be considered a fundamental right to be protected. Since then school finance litigation has relied on state constitutional provisions, which differ greatly. In Colorado, Georgia and New York, for example, state courts have found financing systems constitutional despite disparities in per pupil expenditures. State courts in Arkansas, West Virginia and Wyoming have declared their financing systems unconstitutional.[27]

The debate over equity appears to have produced more results in state legislatures than in state courts. By the end of the 1970s, 30 states had enacted major changes in their school financing system, according to Odden of the Education Commission of the States.[28] Some states increased per pupil expenditures to guarantee a basic level of spending for all students. Others developed equalization formulas that put more state money into poor districts than affluent ones to balance per pupil expenditures. Studies of these reform programs show that they largely succeeded in closing the overall gap in per pupil spending, Odden concludes.

These changes caused state revenues to overtake local revenue as the prime source of school funds *(see chart, p. 15)*. Between 1971-72 and 1981-82, the states' share of school financing rose from 38 percent to 47 percent, while the local share dropped from 55 percent to 45 percent.[29] The shift has created some new problems. Property taxes are a relatively stable source of revenue even during periods of temporary economic downturns. In contrast, the principal sources of state revenues are income and sales taxes, both of which are highly susceptible to swings in the business cycle. During the 1980-82 recession, education budgets were cut in many states as revenues fell. Only recently have state education expenditures begun to recover,

[27] C. Kent McGuire, "School Finance Litigation," Education Commission of the States Issuegram, February 1983.
[28] Allan Odden, "School Finance Reform, Past, Present and Future," Education Commission of the States Issuegram, March 1983, p. 2.
[29] National Center for Education Statistics, "The Condition of Education," 1984, p. 44.

along with the economy. Nonetheless, the increasing role of states in school financing has contributed to a sharp growth in spending per pupil, up from a national average of $911 in 1971-72 to $2,724 a decade later. When adjusted for inflation, the real growth in spending amounted to 34 percent.

Making Schools Work

TWO DEMOGRAPHIC TRENDS could complicate the job of upgrading educational quality. Pupil enrollment, which has steadily declined for more than a decade, is beginning to show signs of growth *(see chart, p. 18)*. Concurrently an over-supply of teachers gradually disappeared, and many educators are predicting a teacher shortage, possibly of serious proportions, by the end of the decade *(see chart, p. 19)*.

Public school enrollment nationwide dropped about 14 percent from a peak of 46.1 million in 1971 to approximately 39.1 million last fall. The enrollment decline forced 5 percent of all public schools (4,652) to close during the 1970s, leaving 85,888 in 1981-82.[30] These aggregate figures mask major differences among regions. The impact of the enrollment slump hit hardest in the Northeast and Midwest, where most states recorded declines greater than the national average. Public school enrollment in Connecticut, Delaware, Rhode Island, South Dakota and the District of Columbia dropped more than 25 percent. In Sun Belt and Western states, enrollment generally fell less than the national average. Eight states — Arizona, Alaska, Florida, Idaho, Nevada, Texas, Utah and Wyoming — registered enrollment growth.

School closings often generated bitter confrontations between neighborhood groups and financially strapped school boards. Many school districts found themselves in the difficult position of closing schools in aging city neighborhoods with fewer and fewer youngsters and building new schools in the suburbs where young couples settled to raise families.

A decline in teaching jobs after 1977 prolonged the teacher surplus that began earlier in the decade. When student enrollment peaked in 1971, colleges graduated nearly two teachers for every job opening. Five years later, colleges still graduated three new teachers for every two jobs. Supply continued to exceed demand into the 1980s but is expected to reach a balance this

---

[30] National Center for Education Statistics, *op. cit.*, p. 3.

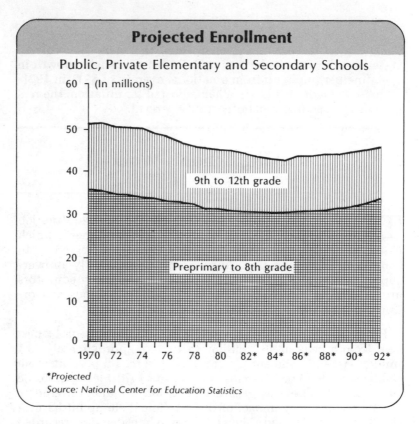

Projected Enrollment

Public, Private Elementary and Secondary Schools

60 (In millions)

9th to 12th grade

Preprimary to 8th grade

1970 72 74 76 78 80 82* 84* 86* 88* 90* 92*

*Projected

Source: National Center for Education Statistics

fall. The National Center for Education Statistics projects a job opening this fall for each of the 146,000 new teacher graduates and anticipates a shortage of teachers the following year.[31] A summer survey by the American Federation of Teachers (AFT) indicates those projections might be conservative. "We traditionally conduct an annual teacher layoff survey, but this year the problem isn't layoffs, it's shortages," says Ruth Whitman, an information specialist at the AFT's Washington office. She noted that increased graduation requirements and reduced student-teacher ratios create new teaching jobs.

Prospects for Severe Teacher Shortage

Whether it arrives this year or next, the teacher shortage is expected to worsen rather than improve. Based on current trends, there will be four jobs available for every three education graduates by the early 1990s. Prospects for a teacher shortage are rooted in demographics. Beginning in 1976, after 19 years of decline, the number of births began to increase as women of the postwar baby-boom generation began having children and as those who had delayed starting families began to do so. Births increased from 3.2 million in 1976 to 3.7 million in

[31] Ibid.

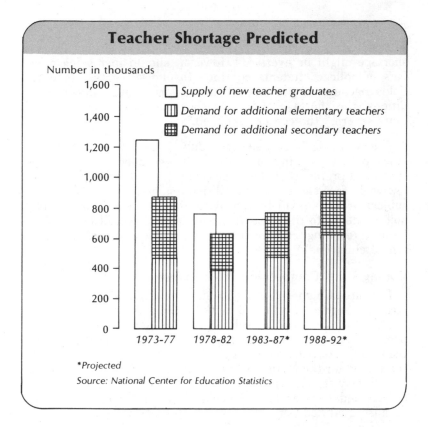

Teacher Shortage Predicted

Number in thousands

- ☐ Supply of new teacher graduates
- ▥ Demand for additional elementary teachers
- ▦ Demand for additional secondary teachers

1973-77 1978-82 1983-87* 1988-92*

*Projected

Source: National Center for Education Statistics

1982 before dropping slightly in 1983.[32] As a result, first-grade classes began getting bigger in 1983. Public school enrollment through the eighth grade is expected to reach 30 million by 1992, an 11 percent increase over the projected 26.6 million enrollment this fall.

Because of these changes, the National Center for Education Statistics projects that the number of public elementary school teaching jobs will begin rising in the fall of 1985 and reach an all-time high of 1.38 million in 1992. These projections assumed that "the total enrollment will rise, teacher-pupil ratios will improve only slightly, and that turnover of teachers will remain constant at an estimated 6 percent." [33]

Whether there will be enough teachers to fill the demand is an open question. Between 1970 and 1982, the percentage of college students majoring in education dropped from 34 to 15 percent, decreasing the number of new teacher graduates from 284,000 to roughly 143,000. If the number of students preparing

---

[32] The Census Bureau projects that annual births will remain at about 3.7 million through the early 1990s and then drop to around 3.4 million through 2080, reflecting a decline in the number of women of childbearing age. See Census Bureau, "Projections of the Population of the United States by Age, Race and Sex: 1983 to 2080," May 1984, p. 10.
[33] National Center For Education Statistics, *op. cit.* p. 9.

to teach rises to about 21 percent in 1992, a serious teacher shortage might be averted. "However, should increasing numbers of college students continue to choose careers in other fields because of perceived better salaries and working conditions, the shortage of new teacher graduates could become quite severe," the center predicted.[34]

This warning is echoed by a July 1984 Rand Corporation study of the teaching profession: "If we choose to ignore the structural problems of the teaching profession, we will in a very few years face shortages of qualified teachers in virtually every subject area. We will be forced to hire the least academically able students to fill these vacancies, and they will become the tenured teaching force for the next two generations of American school children." [35]

Coping With Competition From Industry

The lure of higher-paying jobs in private industry already has created a serious shortage of math and science teachers. "There has been a catastrophic decline in the number of persons prepared to teach science and math, and of those prepared, less than half take teaching positions," the authors of a 1982 study conducted for the National Science Teachers Association found. "Secondary schools are being forced to hire record numbers of unqualified persons for science and math teaching positions because qualified persons cannot be found." [36]

To help solve this problem, Congress in July passed legislation to authorize $965 million in federal funds for math and science teacher training.[37] States also are taking steps to recruit more math and science teachers. The Florida Legislature has passed a bill that will pay teachers to attend summer institutes to obtain math or science certification. New York and North Carolina are among the states offering scholarships and loans to students preparing to teach math or science. For those who become teachers, the loans will be forgiven. Georgia has hired eight unemployed German math teachers to work in its schools, and New York is considering the idea.

Vocational teachers also are in short supply. More than half the high schools surveyed for the American Vocational Association (AVA) in spring 1982 reported problems finding enough

---

[34] *Ibid.*

[35] Linda Darling-Hammond, "Beyond the Commission Reports, The Coming Crisis in Teaching," The Rand Corporation, July 1984, p. 19.

[36] James A. Shymansky and Bill G. Aldridge, "The Teacher Crisis in Secondary School Science and Mathematics," National Science Teachers Association, Washington D.C., 1982, p. 5.

[37] The House Aug. 8 passed and sent to the Senate a bill (HR 4477) to award four-year scholarships to students who graduated in the top 10 percent of their high school classes and intended to become teachers.

Teachers' Views on Reform Measures

A Harris Poll, described as the "first comprehensive report on the attitudes" of American public school teachers found that most of them are "wide open to participating in widespread change and reform within the school system." The survey, released in June, was conducted for the Metropolitan Life Insurance Company.

Responses from the 1,981 teachers interviewed indicated that more than 90 percent supported greater emphasis on basic subjects, higher priority for discipline and safety, tighter graduation requirements and heightened emphasis on computer and foreign language instruction. Seventy-four percent favored increasing homework requirements, but a roughly equal percentage opposed a longer school day or year.

On issues concerning the teaching profession, 87 percent favored career ladders that combine more responsibility with more pay. Seventy-one percent said merit pay could work if there were an objective standard on which a teacher's performance could be judged. But 59 percent rated merit pay an ineffective way to attract and retain good teachers. A slightly higher percentage would not allow school districts to recruit new teachers from among talented college graduates who are not certified to teach.

A majority of teachers also said they were underpaid, burdened with too much administrative work and without sufficient support from parents or the community. A majority — 53 percent — would not advise a young person to pursue a career in teaching.

trade and industrial teachers.[38] One in four said they had trouble hiring teachers for their health occupations, agriculture and technical courses. Low salaries were identified as the major barrier to recruiting. "When graduates of these programs go out and make more money than their instructors, you cannot expect to solve this problem," said Gene Bottoms, AVA's executive director.

The academic qualifications of college students entering teaching is of concern to many education officials. Nationwide, prospective teachers test below the national average in math and verbal skills on standardized college entrance exams. Several states, including New Jersey and Texas, are taking a controversial approach to upgrading the academic quality of its teachers. Their proposed solution is to waive teacher-training requirements to attract top liberal arts graduates who otherwise would not enter teaching. The New Jersey Board of Education is expected to approve a plan in September that would allow schools to hire anyone with a bachelor's degree provided they

---

[38] Orville Nelson, "Characteristics and Needs of Area Vocational Schools," Center for Vocational, Technical and Adult Education, University of Wisconsin at Stout, 1982.

pass a standardized test in the subject area to be taught. These provisional teachers would earn full certification after one year of successful, supervised teaching.

Renewed Confidence in Public Education

The current push for educational improvement comes at a time when researchers are reaching agreement on what works in the classroom. During much of the past decade, a cloud of pessimism hung over public education as researchers postulated that schools and teachers — no matter how well equipped — could do little to overcome the ill effects of poverty, parental neglect and broken homes. This view stemmed largely from two influential books: James Coleman's report on *Equality of Educational Opportunity* (1966) and Christopher Jenck's *Inequality: A Reassessment of the Effect of Family and Schooling in America* (1972). Coleman concluded that a child's ability to learn depended more on his socioeconomic background than what happened in the classroom. After reassessing Coleman's data and a mass of other statistical evidence, Jencks concluded that "the character of a school's output depends largely on a single input, namely the characteristics of the entering children. Everything else — the school budget, its policies, the characteristics of the teachers — is either secondary or completely irrelevant." [39]

In following years, however, new research began to indicate that schools do make a difference. It wasn't enough to show that individual student test scores improved with proper instruction. The larger issue was why students with similar socioeconomic backgrounds did better academically at some schools than at others. Since the late 1970s a consensus has emerged that a schoolwide spirit of commitment — widely referred to as school "ethos" — is necessary for academic success.

British researchers, led by Michael Rutter, popularized the idea of school ethos with publication of *Fifteen Thousand Hours* (1979), a study of 12 inner-London schools. They found that students at some schools exhibited better behavior and scored higher on tests than would be expected, given the students' socioeconomic backgrounds. The secret, the researchers said, was that principals at those schools laid down clear guidelines and monitored teachers' work closely. In addition, teachers expected high performance from their students and rewarded hard work.

The Washington, D.C., schools are an example of how "ethos" has worked, says Denis P. Doyle, director of education policy studies for the American Enterprise Institute. The school sys-

---

[39] Christopher Jencks, *Inequality*, Basic Books, 1972, p. 256.

tem, which is 94 percent black and has many youngsters from poor families, instituted a rigorous back-to-basics curriculum in 1976 to combat low achievement test scores. In the fall of 1980, the system began requiring students to demonstrate mastery of basic math and reading skills to earn promotion to the next grade. The following year third-graders exceeded national averages in reading and math for the first time. Sixth-graders surpassed national averages in both areas in 1982. Scores for both grades have remained above national norms.

A 1982 study by Coleman, Thomas Hoffer and Sally Kilgore tended to support the "ethos" theory, with emphasis on the importance of discipline. In *High School Achievement: Public, Catholic and Private Schools Compared*, the researchers identified two primary reasons why American private school students scored higher on achievement tests than public school students when students of similar backgrounds were compared: private schools demanded more homework, better attendance and higher academic goals. And they enforced strict discipline. "Thus, achievement and discipline are intimately intertwined, and it is no accident that . . . where one is high, the other is high as well," the researchers said.[40]

Discipline remains a significant problem for the public schools. For a number of years, parents interviewed by the Gallup Poll have put lack of discipline at the top of their list of complaints about schools. Teachers interviewed for a Metropolitan Life survey ranked discipline their fourth greatest problem, behind inadequate financial support, student apathy and overcrowded classrooms.[41] Albert Shanker, president of the American Federation of Teachers, warned in an Aug. 12 *New York Times* column that "unless this issue is dealt with, the public support for public schools that this year's Gallup Poll shows is going to vanish."

On a more optimistic note, Denis Doyle contends that "given the right supervisory back-up, teachers who cherish their subject, scorn sloth, reward effort, punish indiscipline, work their students to the bone, and assign lots of homework (and take the time to correct it), can raise the achievement of any student from any neighborhood, even in schools that lack computer terminals, large libraries, and unscarred furniture."[42] The question is whether the public school system can meet such high expectations.

---

[40] James Colemen, Thomas Hoffer and Sally Kilgore, *High School Achievement: Public, Catholic and Private Schools Compared*," Basic Books Inc., 1982, p. 187.

[41] The survey, conducted by Louis Harris and Associates for the Metropolitan Life Insurance Company, was released in June 1984.

[42] Denis P. Doyle, "Window of Opportunity," *The Wilson Quarterly*, New Year's 1984, p. 91.

Selected Bibliography

Books

Coleman, James, Thomas Hoffer and Sally Kilgore, *High School Achievement, Public, Catholic and Private Schools Compared*, Basic Books Inc., 1982.

Jencks, Christopher, *Inequality, A Reassessment of the Effect of Family and Schooling in America*, Basic Books Inc., 1972.

Ravitch, Diane, *The Troubled Crusade, American Education 1945-1980*, Basic Books Inc., 1983.

Rutter, Michael, Barbara Maughan, Peter Mortimore, Janet Ouston, *Fifteen Thousand Hours*, Harvard University Press, 1979.

Articles

Doyle, Denis P., "Window of Opportunity," *Wilson Quarterly*, New Year's 1984.

Odden, Allan, "Financing Educational Excellence," *Phi Delta Kappan*, January 1984.

Reports and Studies

Bridges, Edwin M., and Barry Groves, "Managing the Incompetent Teacher," Institute for Research on Educational Finance and Governance, Stanford University, 1984.

Census Bureau "Projections of the Population of the United States by Age, Sex and Race: 1983 to 2080," Series P-25, No. 952, May 1984.

Darling-Hammond, Linda, "Beyond the Commission Reports, The Coming Crisis in Teaching," The Rand Corporation, 1984.

Editorial Research Reports: "Teachers: The Push for Excellence," 1984 Vol. I, p. 291; "Illiteracy in America," 1983 Vol. I, p. 475; "Post-Sputnik Education," 1982 Vol. II, p. 653.

Hatry, Harry P., and John M. Greiner, "Issues in Teacher Incentive Plans," The Urban Institute, Washington, D.C., Jan. 10, 1984.

"The Metropolitan Life Survey of the American Teacher," conducted for the Metropolitan Life Insurance Co. by Louis Harris and Associates Inc., June 1984.

National Center for Education Statistics, "The Condition of Education, 1984 Edition," 1984.

National Commission on Excellence in Education, "The Nation Responds," May 1984.

National Education Association, "Teacher Supply and Demand in the Public Schools, 1981-82," Washington, D.C., August 1983.

Rosenholtz, Susan J., "Political Myths About Reforming the Teaching Profession," Education Commission of the States, July 1984.

Task Force on Education for Economic Growth, "Action in the States," Education Commission of the States, Denver, July 1984.

Thompson, John A., "Cost Factors of Paying Teachers for Performance," Education Commission of the States, May 1984.

Graphics: Cover illustration by Art Director Richard Pottern; graphics pp. 15, 18, 19 by Kathleen Ossenfort; photos pp. 5, 13 courtesy of American Federation of Teachers.

COLLEGES
IN THE 1980s

by

Roger Thompson

July 27
1984

COLLEGES IN THE 1980s

COLLEGE ISN'T WHAT it used to be. No longer is it a bastion for 18- to 22-year-old white males from upper-income families. Most college students now are women. Most freshmen are enrolled in two-year community colleges, the low-budget newcomer to postsecondary education. Students older than age 25 account for more than one-third of all college enrollments. Largely because of this older group, 40 percent of all students now are part time. Enrollment of blacks and other minorities grew faster over the last decade than any other segment of the campus population, accounting for one out of every seven students.[1]

While these figures represent historic changes in American higher education, they amount to little more than statistical curiosities to parents struggling to cope with figures of another sort: the spiraling cost of their children's college education. The National Center for Education Statistics estimated the average cost for a resident student at a public, four-year college in the 1983-84 school year to be about $3,200. The comparable estimate for the average private college was $7,500.[2] Costs for the 1984-85 academic year are expected to rise 7-9 percent, an improvement over double-digit increases of the past three years. Still, the projected increase is double the inflation rate, which registered 3.7 percent for the year ending in June.

College administrators say tuition and fees have risen sharply in the 1980s to compensate for the inflation of the 1970s that outpaced increases in the cost of college. Reagan administration cutbacks in higher education aid programs have placed additional pressure on parents and students whose federal grants and loans have been reduced or lost altogether. The College Board estimated that the value of all student aid, adjusted for inflation, dropped 21 percent between 1980-81 and 1983-84.[3]

The upward pressure on tuition costs will intensify if anticipated enrollment drops materialize over the next decade at the

---

[1] W. Vance Grant and Thomas D. Snyder, *Digest of Educational Statistics 1983-84*, National Center for Education Statistics, 1984.

[2] National Center for Education Statistics, *The Condition of Education 1984*, 1984, p. 82.

[3] Donald A. Gillespie and Nancy Carlson, "Trends in Student Aid: 1963 to 1983," The College Board, 1983, p. 19. The College Board provides tests and other educational services to students, secondary schools and colleges.

nation's 3,111 postsecondary institutions.[4] The Census Bureau projects a 26 percent drop in the number of 18-year-olds, who continue to make up the majority of college freshmen, between 1979 and 1994. Fewer students would force institutions to raise tuition to make up for lost revenue. Administrators have been surprised and relieved that total enrollment of both full- and part-time students at four- and two-year institutions grew from 12.1 million in 1980-81 to 12.5 million in 1983-84.

Still, it is widely believed that enrollment cannot continue to defy demographics. Because roughly half of all 18-year-olds do not attend college, educators expect the 26 percent drop in their numbers to result in a 15 percent decline in nationwide post-secondary enrollment by the mid-1990s. Some experts predict that 150 to 200 small, liberal arts colleges will go out of business because of the enrollment slump. After 1994, the 18-year-old population — and college enrollment — should climb again as children whose parents comprised the post-World War II baby boom reach college age.

College Costs and Inflation in the 1980s

College costs have risen sharply in recent years, mostly due to inflation.[5] The average cost of attending a public college doubled in 10 years, rising from $1,506 in 1973-74 to an estimated $3,160 in 1983-84, according to the National Center for Education Statistics *(see chart, p. 29)*. The figures for a private college rose from $3,040 to an estimated $7,540.[6] Books, transportation and personal expenses push these averages higher.

At least one study challenges the view that those sharp rises in tuition imposed an increasing financial burden on most families. An Educational Testing Service (ETS) study concluded that "college costs as a percentage of median family income showed little change or actually decreased at most institutions" during the 1970s. "These figures are significant because they suggest that current public discussion may be overstating the problem of rising college costs," wrote ETS researchers Terry W. Hartle and Richard Wabnick.[7] In an interview, Wabnick said the finding "was surprising to a lot of people." Stories about high costs tend to be about Ivy League schools such as

---

[4] 1,887 four-year and 1,224 two-year institutions were operating in 1982-83, the last year for which figures are available from the National Center for Education Statistics.

[5] The American Council on Education found that average college costs — total tuition, fees, room, board, and other personal college expenses — rose 50.8 percent from 1977 through 1982 while inflation as measured by the Consumer Price Index rose 59.4 percent. See Cathy Henderson, "College Costs: Recent Trends, Likely Future," *Policy Brief*, American Council on Education, July 1983, p. 2.

[6] National Center for Education Statistics, *op. cit.*

[7] Terry W. Hartle and Richard Wabnick, "Are College Costs Rising?" *Journal of Contemporary Studies*, spring 1983, p. 64. Persons quoted in this report were interviewed by the author unless otherwise noted.

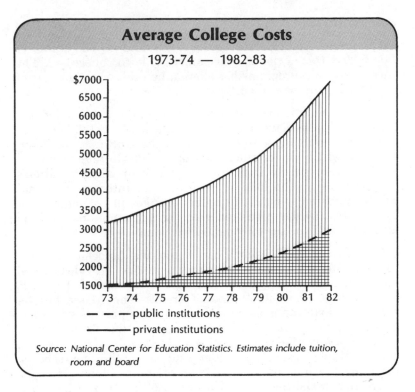

Average College Costs
1973-74 — 1982-83

- - - public institutions
——— private institutions

Source: National Center for Education Statistics. Estimates include tuition, room and board

Harvard, which will charge $14,100 for tuition, fees, room and board next year. "That is where a lot of the perception about high college costs comes from," Wabnick added.

What might have been true in the 1970s apparently is not holding for the early 1980s. A study conducted by the College Board indicates that since 1981 college costs have risen more rapidly than family income, making college "relatively more difficult for families to afford in the 1980s."[8] Since 1981, the rate of annual increase in the Consumer Price Index (CPI) has fallen from 10.4 percent to less than 4 percent, while average college costs rose more than 10 percent annually through 1983-84. During this period, the study found that disposable family income, adjusted for inflation, remained stagnant while total student aid dropped 21 percent, due largely to cuts at the federal level.

Innovative Plans to Ease Tuition Burden

Despite the cuts, federal aid remains the primary source of help for financially strapped students and their parents (see p. 35). However, many colleges have developed new ways to help parents cope with costs. Innovative plans for student aid surged during the early years of the Reagan administration when the president "announced he was going to take a meat ax to college

[8] Gillespie and Carlson, *op. cit.* p. vi.

aid programs," said Robert Leider of Alexandria, Va., author of
Don't Miss Out, a popular consumer guide to college aid. The
pace of new aid programs has slowed, he said, now that fear of
drastic aid cuts has eased.[9]

Based on a nationwide survey completed in June, Leider said
the only new financing idea from colleges for next fall is the so-
called "adjustable-rate tuition loan" at the University of Pennsylvania, which works much like an adjustable rate mortgage.
Parents who borrow from the university for their children's
education repay the loan at below-market interest rates that
will be adjusted annually to reflect changes in commercial interest rates. Leider predicted that the adjustable-rate tuition
loan soon will spread to other institutions.

In addition, the Student Loan Marketing Association (Sally
Mae), the federally chartered corporation that provides capital
for student loan programs, has agreed to extend Brandeis
University a $2.5-million line of credit. The Massachusetts
school will loan the money to middle-income parents who want
to prepay four years of tuition as a hedge against future tuition
increases. Sally Mae is negotiating with several other colleges to
start a similar program, Leider said. Several other schools,
including Washington University in St. Louis, Johns Hopkins
University in Baltimore, the University of Southern California,
and Averett and Lynchburg colleges in Virginia also offer pre-
payment options.

Other innovative financing plans developed over the past
several years include:

● Installment plans: Most colleges now allow parents to
spread payments over the school year. Some schools offer
a discount if the total year's tuition is paid in a lump
sum.

● Deferred repayment: Parents may repay college costs over
25 to 30 years. Yale University uses such a plan.

● Low-interest loan programs: Some colleges offer low-cost
loans to parents. Dickinson College in Pennsylvania uses its
endowment to finance the loans. Dartmouth College raises its
loan funds from tax-exempt bonds.

● Middle-income assistance programs: These programs offer
scholarships and loans specifically to students whose families
may not qualify for federal aid programs.

● Lower tuition: Biscayne College in Miami, Fla., cut tuition

---

[9] Leider conducts annual surveys of college and university costs and aid programs for his
publication, *Don't Miss Out*, which may be found in many libraries and loan offices or
purchased directly from Octameron, P.O. Box 3437, Alexandria, Va. 22302.

Postsecondary School Revenues, 1980-81

(in billions of dollars)

Source	All Schools		Public		Private	
Tuition, fees	$13.8	21.0%	$ 5.6	12.9%	$8.2	36.6%
Federal government	9.7	14.9	5.5	12.8	4.2	18.8
State government	20.1	30.7	19.7	45.6	.4	1.9
Local government	1.8	2.7	1.6	3.8	.2	.7
Private giving	3.2	4.8	1.1	2.5	2.1	9.3
Endowments	1.4	2.1	.2	.5	1.1	5.1
Sales, services*	13.7	20.9	8.5	19.6	5.2	23.3
Other	1.9	3.0	1.1	2.4	.9	4.2

* Includes educational activities, auxiliary enterprises and hospitals.

Source: Grant and Snyder, Digest of Education Statistics, 1983-84

$400 in September 1982, advertised extensively and increased enrollment by 93 percent.

New Sources of Income for Institutions

Tuitions may be rising, but in neither private nor public schools do they cover the costs of education. Public institutions get nearly half of their annual operating revenues from state governments, compared with about 13 percent raised from tuition. For private institutions, tuition is the largest single source of revenue, but it accounts for just 37 percent of total revenues. For both public and private institutions, federal dollars are important. The federal government grants research contracts, supports the purchase of certain kinds of educational equipment and supplies, loans funds for construction and gives special grants to developing institutions *(see table, above)*.

Fund raising has always been crucial to the survival of private institutions. But it is an area that public institutions in large numbers have only recently begun to explore. A decade of financial uncertainty caused by inflation, recession, tight state budgets and federal aid cuts have forced many public colleges to turn to private giving as a supplementary funding source. "There were a great number of public institutions that never did [any fund raising] before. Now more of them are getting into it. They just aren't going to be able to keep going back to state legislatures for more and more funds," said Anne F. Decker, vice president of the Council for Financial Aid to Education in New York City.

Much of the private money for higher education flows into endowments, permanent accounts that generate income to support a variety of programs, or into special funds used to enhance programs or pay for one-time construction projects. The market value of public institutions' endowments nearly doubled between 1971 and 1981 to $4.2 billion, while the value of private institutions' funds climbed about 40 percent to $19.3 billion.[10] Eighty-three percent (1,162) of the nation's private colleges had endowment funds in 1981 compared with about 40 percent (600) of the public institutions.

Total endowments for all institutions accounted for only 2.1 percent of revenue in the 1980-81 school year, although some schools obtained 20 percent or more of their revenues from endowments. Only one public institution, the University of Texas at Austin, ranks in the top 10 institutions with the largest endowments.[11] The Texas university in 1981 held a $1.4 billion endowment that accounted for about one-third of the endowments held by all public institutions.

Non-endowment fund raising also has increased rapidly for public institutions. In academic year 1972-73, public four-year colleges received 22 percent of all private giving to higher education. The figure rose to 31 percent by 1982-83, Decker said. Among the public institutions reporting the highest amounts of voluntary giving for current operating expenditures in 1982-83 were the University of Minnesota, $55.2 million; Texas A&M University, $33.9 million; University of Wisconsin-Madison, $33.2 million; the University of California at Los Angeles, $32.6 million; the University of Michigan, $31.1 million; and the University of Illinois, $22.3 million.[12]

Many large colleges also undertake private enterprises to raise needed capital. In recent years, a small school, Arkansas College at Batesville, has attracted national attention for its aggressive pursuit of profit-making ventures. In 1982, the Presbyterian school with an enrollment of 700 formed a private corporation, which has purchased a major supermarket in Huntsville, Ala., and acquired a large tract of land suitable for development.

The corporation also has plans to operate a small hydroelectric generating plant. "All these projects are long term. We don't expect to make a fast buck," said Dan C. West, the college president. He said any profits from the business ventures would be used to hold down tuition. "You can only raise your tuition so much before you begin to price yourself out of the market," West added.

---

[10] *Digest of Education Statistics 1983-84,* p. 150.

[11] The other nine are Harvard University ($1.7 billion), Yale University ($799 million), Stanford University ($688 million), Princeton University ($686 million), University of Rochester ($501 million), Massachusetts Institute of Technology ($500 million), University of Chicago ($397 million), Rice University ($391 million) and Columbia University, main branch ($360 million).

[12] "Voluntary Support of Education 1982-83," Council For Financial Aid to Education (1983).

Federal Influence

THE FEDERAL GOVERNMENT is by far the largest source of student aid. Its grant and loan programs generated 78 percent of the estimated $16.1 billion in aid available to students in 1983-84, according to the College Board *(see chart, p. 35)*.[13] But federal dominance is a fairly recent occurrence. Before the 1960s, aid generally took the form of scholarships awarded by colleges and universities. Federal assistance was limited largely to the G.I. Bill, which put thousands of World War II and Korean War veterans through college during the 1950s. Spending for veterans' education, however, gradually diminished as benefits were used or expired.

The era of broad government commitment to student aid can be traced to the Soviet launching of the first satellite, Sputnik I, in the fall of 1957. The shock to Americans led to anguished warnings that the United States was falling behind in scientific fields and a parade of witnesses offered to congressional committees a myriad of proposals for improving higher education.[14] The result was passage of the National Defense Education Act of 1958. Its main provision set up the first federal low-cost loan program for needy students *(see box, p. 36)*.

In 1963 Congress authorized grants and loans for construction and improvement of academic facilities at both private and public colleges, and in 1964 it established the College Work-Study program as part of the Economic Opportunity Act, President Johnson's anti-poverty legislation. With a strong push from Johnson, a former school teacher, and broad bipartisan support, Congress the following year enacted the Higher Education Act of 1965. The measure was revolutionary in several aspects. For the first time in U.S. history, the federal government approved outright grants to undergraduates. The act also established a student loan program (now known as Guaranteed Student Loans) in which the federal government subsidized the interest payments and insured the loans in case of default. In a separate action, Congress extended the Social Security student benefit program to cover college-age students. Such benefits went to the children of deceased, retired or disabled parents eligible for Social Security.

Push to Open Federal Aid to Middle Class

Federal higher education programs were substantially restructured with passage of the Education Amendments of

---

[13] Gillespie and Carlson, *op. cit.*, p. 5.
[14] For background, see "College Financing," *E.R.R.* 1971 Vol. I, pp. 141-164.

1972. Added to the roster of federal student aid programs were Basic Educational Opportunity Grants, renamed Pell grants in 1980, which entitled any college student to a grant of $1,400 minus the amount the student's family could reasonably be expected to contribute to the student's education.[15] Congress also created the State Student Incentive Grant program that provided matching funds for states to set up grant programs for needy students. All 50 states have established such programs.[16]

It was during the 1970s that pressure began to mount to open federal student aid programs to students from middle-income families. The combination of inflation and recession that occurred during the 1970s pushed college costs up at a fast pace. Between 1966 and 1976 higher education costs went up 77 percent. But most middle-income families remained ineligible for federal aid programs, which were intended to help the neediest students. "Increasingly, middle-income families, not just lower-income families, are being stretched to their financial limits by these new and growing costs of a college or university education," President Carter said in 1978.

One avenue of relief favored by many parents and private institutions was a tuition tax credit. In 1978, both the House and Senate approved legislation creating tax credits for college tuition. But the bill, which was opposed by the Carter administration and public colleges and universities, died when the House insisted the credits also be given to parents who sent their children to private and parochial elementary and secondary schools.[17]

In its place, Congress approved the Middle Income Student Assistance Act, which made Pell grants available to students from families with incomes of about $27,000. The income limit had been approximately $15,000. The measure also opened the College Work-Study program to students from families earning more than $16,000 and lifted income restrictions on the Guaranteed Student Loan program, making higher-income families eligible for the first time for interest subsidies. Passage of the Middle Income Student Assistance Act quickly led to large increases in Pell grants and guaranteed loans as the new middle-income constituency took advantage of the government programs. The number of Pell grant recipients grew from 1.9 mil-

---

[15] Sen. Claiborne Pell, D-R.I., chairman of the Senate Education Subcommittee from 1969 to 1981, was the original sponsor of the basic educational opportunity grants.

[16] Robert H. Fenske and Joseph D. Boyd, "State Need-Based College Scholarship and Grant Programs: A Study of Their Development, 1969-1980," The College Board, 1981, p. 4.

[17] The Reagan administration's proposal to establish tuition tax credits for parents who send their children to private elementary and secondary schools was defeated, 59-38, last November by the Senate. For background, see "Tuition Tax Credits," E.R.R., 1981 Vol. II, pp. 595-610.

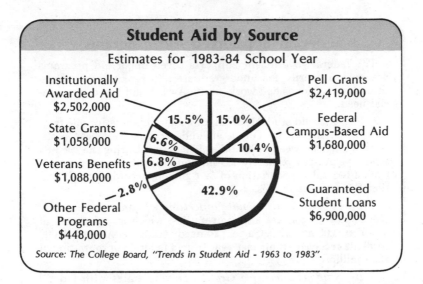

Student Aid by Source

Estimates for 1983-84 School Year

Institutionally
Awarded Aid
$2,502,000

State Grants
$1,058,000

Veterans Benefits
$1,088,000

Other Federal
Programs
$448,000

Pell Grants
$2,419,000

Federal
Campus-Based Aid
$1,680,000

Guaranteed
Student Loans
$6,900,000

15.5% 15.0%

6.6%

10.4%

6.8%

2.8%

42.9%

Source: The College Board, "Trends in Student Aid - 1963 to 1983".

lion in 1977-78 to 2.6 million by 1980-81. The number of students receiving guaranteed loans swelled over the same period from one million to three and one-half million.

Declining Student Aid Levels Under Reagan

President Reagan entered office in 1981 determined to cut the federal government's spending on domestic programs including higher education. Underlying the administration's thrust was the belief that federally funded student aid programs were replacing parental support. "What people haven't been willing to admit is that parental contributions had been going down and that federal dollars were being used to supplant parental contributions," said Edward M. Elmendorf, an assistant secretary for education. Representatives of higher education say cuts in federal student aid hurt those most dependent on it. "The administration has attempted to restrict availability of student aid at every step of the way, and this has affected the neediest families and the middle class," said Charles B. Saunders Jr., vice president of governmental relations for the Washington-based American Council on Education.

Congress agreed to some important changes early in 1981. These included a phase-out of the Social Security student benefits to college-age students, eligibility limits on the Guaranteed Student Loan program and spending ceilings on most other student aid programs for fiscal years 1982 through 1984. Additional spending cuts proposed in late 1981 and 1982 ran into a wall of opposition from the higher education community, parents, students and Congress.[18] No major changes were

---

[18] Congress in 1982 did vote to bar federal student aid to male college students who failed to register with the Selective Service. The Supreme Court upheld the law in 1984 in the case of *Selective Service System v. Minnesota Public Interest Research Group.*

Federally Supported Aid Programs

The federal government supports seven major aid programs designed primarily for undergraduates: three kinds of grants, three types of loans and work-study. Awards are based on financial need.

Pell Grants aid students from low- and moderate-income families by paying up to half of an undergraduate's college costs. Grants range between $200 and $1,900 a year. During the 1983-84 school year, approximately 2.3 million students received grants from a federal appropriation of $2.4 billion, according to Education Department figures.

Supplemental Educational Opportunity Grants channel federal money to colleges and universities, which award grants of between $200 and $2,000 a year to needy students. About 545,000 students received grants last year from a federal appropriation of $355 million.

State Student Incentive Grants provide states with federal funds that they must match dollar for dollar. Most states over-match, some at a ratio of 90 to 1. Approximately 240,000 needy students received grants last year. The federal appropriation totaled $60 million.

Guaranteed Student Loans allow students to borrow up to $2,500 a year from private sources — banks, savings and loans or credit unions — at a below-market interest rate, currently 8 percent. The federal government pays the difference between the student rate and the higher market rate and guarantees the loan against default. Repayment is deferred until the student graduates or leaves school. Students from families with an adjusted gross income in excess of $30,000 must demonstrate a need for loan assistance. About 2.8 million students received loans last year. The government appropriated $3.1 billion to cover interest payments and administrative costs.

National Direct Student Loans provide federal money to institutions to make low-interest loans to needy students. The current interest rate is 5 percent. Repayment is deferred until the student graduates or leaves school. The program served about 876,000 students last year from a federal appropriation of $179 million.

Parent Loans for Undergraduate Students permit parents to take out federally guaranteed loans of up to $3,000 a year for five years for their children's education. The government also subsidizes the interest rate when it exceeds 12 percent. Repayment begins within 60 days after the loan is made and may extend up to 10 years. About 100,000 loans were made last year.

College Work-Study provides federally funded part-time jobs to qualified college students. Students typically work 10 to 15 hours a week during the academic year and are paid at least the federal minimum wage of $3.35 an hour. Approximately 876,000 students participated in the program last year. Federal funding totaled $590 million.

adopted. Among those killed were proposals to require students to pay interest on their college loans while they were in school and to pay market rates on loans instead of the subsidized rate.

Rather than advocate further deep cuts in college aid, the president in his fiscal 1984 budget pushed for a new "Student Assistance Improvement Amendments" package. In a March 17, 1983, message to Congress, Reagan said the amendments would "redirect the present student aid system from one in which some students can get federal grants without contributing any of their own money, to a system which begins with self-help, with parents and students shouldering their fair share of the cost of education before federal grants are made." The administration also proposed creation of so-called Educational Savings accounts, which would allow families to put aside $1,000 annually per child with no federal taxes on the interest or dividends earned. Congress gave no serious consideration to the proposals.

Although the president called for passage of his self-help plan in his fiscal 1985 budget, most congressional observers believe there will be no significant changes in aid to higher education this year due to the presidential election. The next confrontation over student aid is not likely until Congress debates renewal of the Higher Education Act. The law expires Sept. 30, 1985, but has an automatic two-year extension if it is not reauthorized by then.

Drop in Low-Income Student Enrollment

Saunders of the American Council on Education notes that the basic structure of federal student aid programs remains unchanged despite the assault of the early 1980s.[19] But he and others say the aid cuts are responsible both for a shift in emphasis from grants to loans and for declining enrollment among students from low-income families.

Among students enrolled at private colleges, the number receiving Pell grants decreased from 66 percent in 1979-80 to 34 percent in 1983-84, according to a survey by the National Institute of Independent Colleges and Universities. Conversely, the number receiving loans increased from 23 percent to 59 percent.[20] Low- and middle-income students at private schools have "never before been burdened with this much debt," said Julianne Thrift, the institute's executive director.

---

[19] Charles B. Saunders Jr., "Reshaping Federal Aid to Higher Education," in *The Crisis in Higher Education,* Joseph Fromkin, ed., 1983.

[20] National Institute of Independent Colleges and Universities, "Who Gets Student Aid: A 1983-84 Snapshot," July 1984. The institute is the research arm of the National Association of Independent Colleges and Universities.

Administrators say they are seeing a disturbing drop in the number of middle-income students enrolling in private institutions and a sharp overall decline in low-income student enrollment. The National Institute found a 39 percent falloff in enrollment among students from families earning less than $24,000 between 1979-80 and 1981-82. Furthermore, in the past two years, minority students enrolled at public colleges have received a smaller share of state and federal aid, down from 35 percent to 28 percent, according to Jacob Stampen. An associate professor of education at the University of Wisconsin in Madison, Stampen conducts annual student aid surveys for public colleges.

Facing the Future

NO MATTER HOW HIGH colleges boost tuition and fees or what the level of government aid, enrollment is the ultimate measure of an institution's financial health. Enrollment more than doubled from 1965, when the first members of the postwar baby-boom generation matriculated, through last year — from 5.9 million to an estimated 12.5 million. But the number of 18-year-olds peaked in 1979 at 4.3 million and is expected to drop to 3.2 million by 1994 before going up again.[21]

Thus far, the drop in college-age teen-agers has been offset by a number of factors, including the economy. Recession and 10 percent unemployment in the early 1980s contributed to increased enrollments. "In times of economic difficulty, when jobs are scarce, enrollments always go up," said Saunders. "Older people go back to retrain for new jobs." This is especially true for two-year community colleges and technical schools because of their low cost and orientation toward part-time enrollment.

Conversely, the economic recovery that began at the end of 1982 has been good for private institutions, where high costs depress enrollment during a recession. According to the National Association of Independent Colleges and Universities, enrollment last year rebounded from a 1.1 percent drop in the fall of 1982. "Parents now have a greater sense of assurance that they can make the financial arrangements necessary to cover

---

[21] The Northeast and North Central states are expected to be hardest hit with projected declines in the 18-year-old population of 40 percent and 32 percent respectively. By contrast, the Southeast and South Central regions will experience projected declines of 16 percent and 13 percent. See William R. McConnell and Norman Kaufman, "High School Graduates: Projections for the Fifty States (1982-2000)," Western Interstate Commission for Higher Education (1984).

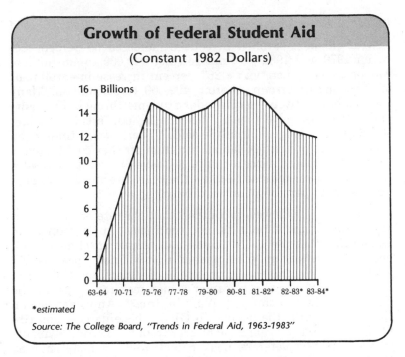

Growth of Federal Student Aid

(Constant 1982 Dollars)

16 ┐ Billions

14 -

12 -

10 -

8 -

6 -

4 -

2 -

0 ┘

63-64   70-71   75-76   77-78   79-80   80-81   81-82*   82-83*   83-84*

*estimated

Source: The College Board, "Trends in Federal Aid, 1963-1983"

the cost of private education," John Phillips, the association's president, said.

It is unclear what roles high school graduation rates, college entry rates and enrollment of older students, especially women, will play in overall enrollment trends. High school graduation rates climbed steadily from 1970 to 1982, supplying an increased pool of potential college applicants. Seventy-one percent of persons 25 years old and over had completed high school in 1982, compared with 55 percent in 1970, according to Census Bureau figures.[22]

Forty-nine percent of the nation's 4.2 million 18-year-olds enrolled in higher education in 1981, up from 46.4 percent the year before, the last years for which figures are available.[23] The growth may have been an aberration produced by the recession of the early 1980s. Whatever the case, even modest growth in the percentage of 18-year-olds entering college helps offset the decline in their numbers. "A 1 percent increase in the college-going rate translates into offsetting a 2 percent drop in college enrollment," said Norman Kaufman.[24]

Many colleges expect increased enrollment of persons over 25. Impressive gains already have been made. The number of 25- to

---

[22] "Population Profile of the United States: 1982," Bureau of the Census, 1983, pp. 20-21.
[23] *Digest of Education Statistics 1983-84*, p. 10, p. 68.
[24] Kaufman is director of Institutional Studies and Analysis at the New York State University Center at Binghamton, N.Y.

34-year-old men enrolled in college increased 55 percent between 1970 and 1982 — from roughly 940,000 to 1.5 million. Among women, there was a 267 percent increase in enrollment of the same age group — from 409,000 to 1.5 million. Many colleges now actively recruit older students through TV, radio and newspaper advertising. "No one is indifferent [to older students] any longer," Phillips said. "There was a time when colleges and universities had all the students they could handle. But not anymore." Urban campuses have the most success in recruiting adult students because they can cater to the needs of professional upgrading and retraining, he added.

Some analysts, however, contend that the rate of increase in adult student enrollment cannot continue. "One reason is an assumption that the sharp increase of female enrollments is a one-time 'catching-up' phenomenon that will not repeat itself," wrote Davd W. Breneman, president of Kalamazoo College in Kalamazoo, Mich., and a former senior research fellow at the Brookings Institution in Washington.[25] Another reason Breneman cites is the decline in GI Bill benefits that contributed substantially to enrollment growth in the 1970s. Payments to Vietnam War veterans peaked in 1975-76 at more than $5 billion and dropped to about $1 billion last year.[26] Rapid growth in the number of part-time students — most of whom are adults — from 2.8 million in 1970 to 5.2. million in 1982, also has slowed in the 1980s.

Many Small Colleges Expected to Close

Even when offsetting factors are considered, the consensus view among educators is that enrollment will decline about 15 percent by the mid-1990s. "Don't forget that the bottoming out point isn't until the 1990s. The demographic trends are overwhelming. They establish a basic pattern. What we don't know yet is the exact effect this trend will have on college enrollment. But it is likely that some [colleges] are going to succumb," Kaufman said.

The National Center for Education Statistics in its 1980 edition of *The Condition of Education* calculated that enrollment shrinkage could close as many as 200 institutions, mostly small, private, four-year, residential colleges. Over a three-year period ending in 1981-82, 17 institutions closed, all of them private, according to the latest figures from the center. Nathan Dickmeyer, an expert in college finances, said recently that he expects an additional 150 to 170 small institutions to fail. "Gen-

[25] David W. Breneman, "The Coming Enrollment Crisis," *Change*, March 1983, p. 17.

[26] Gillespie and Carlson, *op. cit.*, p. 30. The Senate on June 13, 1984, passed an amendment to the defense authorization bill that would revive the GI Bill by offering $500 a month in educational benefits for three years to certain recruits once they have completed military service. The House passed a more generous version on May 31. Differences must be ironed out in conference committee.

erally, they are very small, and located in areas where there is lots of competition," he said.

Least vulnerable are urban campuses that can draw commuter and part-time students and offer night classes. Ivy League and other prestige institutions also seem to be immune to demographic trends. Six of the eight Ivy League schools — Columbia, Cornell, Dartmouth, Princeton, Yale and the University of Pennsylvania — received record numbers of applications for this fall.[27] Other highly regarded schools across the country report a similar surge in applications. "Parents are increasingly perceiving high-quality education as a durable consumer good," said Willis J. Stetson Jr., dean of admissions at the University of Pennsylvania.[28]

Concern over declining enrollment has led an increasing number of colleges to offer large scholarships based on academic achievement, rather than financial need, to lure outstanding students.[29] Such awards represent a break with the dominant philosophy underlying financial assistance for the past 25 years. And it has drawn sharp criticism from some quarters. "Admission is a recognition of merit; aid is based on need," said Joseph P. Case, dean of financial aid at Amherst College. "I believe it [achievement-based aid] is a heinous practice, especially if you're buying students on the one hand and not meeting the needs of others on the other."[30]

Special Problems Faced by Black Colleges

The nation's 102 historically black colleges and universities have a special set of problems to deal with if they are to survive. Black enrollments in postsecondary education increased greatly over the past 20 years, from 274,000 in 1965 to 1.1 million last year. Up to the mid-1960s, the traditionally black institutions provided the mainstay of college opportunity for the nation's blacks. Since then civil rights laws have opened the doors of traditionally white institutions. Today only 17 percent of all black college students attend a predominantly black institution. Most of these schools have managed to hang on, but the future does not look good for many of them, despite a 2.5 percent enrollment increase last year to about 250,000 students.

Many black colleges are in financial trouble primarily because they serve predominantly low-income students, said Samuel I. Myers, president of the Washington-based National Association for Equal Opportunity in Higher Education. Moreover, many

---

[27] Applications to Harvard University were up but did not set a record. Applications to Brown University dropped 4.3 percent.
[28] Quoted in *The New York Times*, Feb. 21, 1984.
[29] Robert Leider, *Don't Miss Out, 1984-85*, p. 52. About 1,000 colleges offer scholarships of all sizes.
[30] Quoted in *The New York Times*, April 25, 1983.

critics say that black colleges are anachronistic now that desegregation has removed their mission. Supporters counter that integration is limited and that black institutions remain the chief source of postsecondary education for blacks, particularly in the South where most of the traditionally black schools are located. Black colleges still confer a disproportionately high 40 percent of all undergraduate degrees awarded to blacks each year.

"Before desegregation, they [black institutions] had a steady flow of students," said Clyde Aveilhe, associate director of the Educational Testing Service office in Washington. "But desegregation has set up a difficult situation for them. To the extent they can show they are quality alternatives, plus offer ethnic and cultural benefits, they can make it." A recent Educational Testing Service report indicates that black colleges do offer quality programs. The report, "Participation of Recent Black College Graduates in the Labor Market and in Graduate Education," concluded that "earning a degree from a black college is not a deterrent to employment opportunities." [31]

Costly Capital Improvements, Salary Needs

For most postsecondary institutions, financial problems lie ahead even if expected enrollment declines fail to develop. High inflation rates during the 1970s forced colleges to allocate a larger share of their budgets for physical plant operations, especially utilities. In an effort to keep tuition increases as low as possible, administrators deferred expensive renovation and repair projects and held faculty raises below the inflation rate.

Harvey Kaiser, an expert in college facility needs, says deferred maintenance has reached crisis proportions: "I estimate that between 40 and 50 billion dollars is needed across the more than 3,000 campuses for renewal and replacement problems of buildings, grounds, facilities and equipment." [32]

Kaiser, vice president of facilities at Syracuse University, estimated that the combined renewal and replacement needs total $70.4 million for an "average" university, $6.3 million for a four-year college and $1.7 million for a two-year college. [33] Kaiser calls on institutions to develop capital improvement plans, but he doubts that most will be up to the financial challenge. "Many institutions have already reduced the size of their operations, reallocated resources internally and retrenched faculty,

[31] Joan C. Baratz and Myra Ficklen, "Participation of Recent Black College Graduates in the Labor Market and in Graduate Education," Educational Testing Service (1983). The report was based on data collected by the National Center for Education Statistics. See also "Plight of America's Black Colleges," *E.R.R.*, 1981 Vol. I, pp. 39-56.
[32] Quoted in *AGB Reports (The Journal of the Association of Governing Boards of Universities and Colleges)*, March/April 1984, p. 7.
[33] Harvey Kaiser, *Crumbling Academe*, 1984, p. 15.

Information Sources for Student Aid

Public libraries and student aid offices stock a number of publications to help students locate sources of financial aid. Among the resources available are:

Annual Register of Grant Support contains more than 2,000 programs providing grant support in various academic areas. Published by Marquis Who's Who Inc., Chicago.

The College Blue Book: Scholarships, Fellowships, Grants, and Loans lists financial aid sources for freshmen through advanced professional training programs. Published by Macmillan Information, New York.

The College Cost Book, 1983-84 lists costs at more than 3,200 institutions and provides information on sources of aid. Published by The College Board, New York.

Financial Aids for Higher Education provides information on more than 4,000 aid sources. Published by William C. Brown Co., Dubuque, Iowa.

staff and programs to shrink the budget base," Kaiser wrote. He predicts that the situation gradually will worsen to the point that the states and federal government will be forced to step in with massive infusions of cash.

The future for faculty is no less troubling. Faculty members lost about 20 percent of their purchasing power during the 1970s due to inflation, said Irving J. Spitzberg Jr., past president of the American Association of University Professors (AAUP). While faculty wage hikes have outpaced inflation for the past three years, the cumulative increase adjusted for inflation amounts to 3.2 percent, according to the AAUP.[34] "At that rate, these people will be retired before they make up for the [income] erosion of the last decade," he said.

He fears that the shrinkage in faculty buying power will undercut the profession. "You have a very large number of the very best students who are deciding not to become faculty because of the erosion in income," Spitzberg said. "It's easy to go through the litany of higher education's problems and come out with a very dark view of the future," he added. "But these are problems with solutions. There are reasonable, affordable solutions. And with a small degree of political leadership at the local, state and federal levels, these problems will be solved."

---

[34] The average faculty salary in 1983-84 was $29,130, according to AAUP figures, ranging from a $37,400 average for professors to a $20,710 average for lecturers.

Selected Bibliography

Books

Breneman, David W., and Susan C. Nelson, *Financing Community Colleges*, Brookings Institution, 1981.
The College Cost Book 1983-84, College Board, 1983.

Articles

Breneman, David W., "The Coming Enrollment Crisis," *Change*, March, 1983.
Chronicle of Higher Education, selected issues.
Hartle, Terry W., and Richard Wabnick, "Are College Costs Rising?" *Journal of Contemporary Studies*, spring 1983.
Henderson, Cathy, "College Costs: Recent Trends, Likely Future," *Policy Brief* (American Council on Education), July 1983.
Saunders, Charles B., "Reshaping Federal Aid to Higher Education," reprint from *The Crisis in Higher Education*, Joseph Froomkin ed., The Academy of Political Science, 1983.

Reports and Studies

"The Annual Report on the Economic Status of the Profession, 1983-84," *Academe* (Bulletin of the American Association of University Professors) July/August 1984.
Baratz, Joan C., and Myra Ficklen, "Participation of Recent Black College Graduates in the Labor Market and in Graduate Education," Educational Policy Research Service (Educational Testing Service), 1983.
Editorial Research Reports: "College Tuition Costs," 1978 Vol. I, p. 143; "College Admissions," 1980 Vol. I, p. 265; "Plight of America's Black Colleges," 1981 Vol. I, p. 39; "Tuition Tax Credits," 1981 Vol. II, p. 593.
Fenske, Robert H., and Joseph D. Boyd, "State Need-Based College Scholarship Programs: A Study of Their Development, 1969-1980," College Board, 1981.
Gillespie, Donald A., and Nancy Carlson, "Trends in Student Aid: 1963 to 1983," College Board, 1983.
Grant, W. Vance, and Thomas D. Snyder, *Digest of Educational Statistics 1983-84*, National Center for Education Statistics, 1983.
McConnell, William R., and Norman Kaufman, "High School Graduates: Projections for the Fifty States (1982-2000)," Western Interstate Commission for Higher Education, Boulder, Colo., 1984.
"Population Profile of the United States: 1982," U.S. Bureau of the Census, Series P-23, No. 130, 1983.
"Tax Breaks for College: Current and Proposed Tax Provisions that Help Families Meet College Costs," College Board, 1984.

Graphics: Cover illustration by George Rebh; graphics on pp. 29, 31, 35, and 39 by Assistant Art Director Robert Redding

TEACHERS
THE PUSH FOR EXCELLENCE

by

Roger Thompson

Apr. 20
1 9 8 4

Editor's Note: Since this report was published, Congress passed legislation authorizing funds to improve the quality of science and mathematics training. The measure, signed by the president Aug. 11, 1984, authorized $350 million in fiscal 1984 and $400 million in fiscal 1985 for state grants for science and math teacher training and retraining. Additionally, $75 million in fiscal 1984 and $140 million in fiscal 1985 were earmarked for National Science Foundation grants for teacher training institutes, development of instructional materials and joint projects between schools and private business to improve math, science and engineering education.

TEACHERS
THE PUSH FOR EXCELLENCE

COMPLAINTS ABOUT public schools are legion: students who cannot read or write, achievement test scores on the skids, poor discipline, relaxed standards and lowered expectations. Move to the head of the list complaints about the nation's 2.1 million public school teachers. Teachers are not newcomers to criticism. Their competence has come under increasing public scrutiny since the late 1970s as states began requiring prospective teachers to pass skills tests to prove their basic ability.

But now teachers are *the* focus of debate on the quality of education. Several states, most notably Arkansas, California, Florida and Tennessee, have enacted in the last year controversial educational reform packages with a heavy emphasis on improving teaching. Others, like Virginia and North Carolina, are testing similar plans. In general, these plans are designed to make it tougher to become a teacher and more financially rewarding for those who do, especially for the most talented. To date, most activity has been concentrated in Southern states, where schools have been rated among the poorest in the country in terms of state financial assistance and student performance *(see tables, pp. 53, 61).*

Why the burst of interest in teachers? A number of recent reports concluded that teachers hold the key to upgrading the disappointing quality of American public schools *(see box, p. 49).* The National Commission on Excellence in Education touched off the teacher debate on April 26, 1983. "If an unfriendly foreign power had attempted to impose on America the mediocre educational performance that exists today, we might have viewed it as an act of war," the commission concluded in its report, "A Nation at Risk: The Imperative for Educational Reform." [1] The report stressed that the decline of America's smokestack industries and the rise of foreign, high-tech economic competition make education all the more vital as the foundation for a secure future. It is up to classroom teachers to lay that foundation, the commission said, but under current conditions there is reason to despair. The commission found:

---

[1] The 18-member commission was appointed by Education Secretary T. H. Bell on Aug. 26, 1981. Made up primarily of educators, the commission was chaired by David P. Gardner, then the president of the University of Utah.

● Too many teachers are being drawn from the bottom quarter of graduating high school and college students *(see p. 57)*.

● The teacher preparation curriculum is weighted heavily with courses in educational methods at the expense of courses in subjects to be taught.

● The average public school teacher's salary is only $17,000, forcing many teachers to take part-time jobs to supplement their income and discouraging others from becoming teachers *(see table, p. 53)*.

● There are severe shortages of math and science teachers, and other shortages soon may develop as the student population rebounds from years of decline and again grows in the late 1980s *(see p. 55)*.

Changes Recommended by Study Groups

The commission offered seven recommendations to "make teaching a more rewarding and respected profession." These included raising teacher training standards, making salaries competitive with those in private enterprise, creating career ladders that pay more to teachers assuming additional responsibilities, and offering performance-based or merit pay that would reward superior teachers. It also urged longer school days and years, more homework, stricter discipline, and stiffer graduation requirements — including four years of English courses, three years each of math, science and social studies plus one semester of computer studies.

Critics say the report overstated the deficiencies of American public schools, but they agree that it served the important purpose of catching the public's attention.[2] "The report was a hand grenade rolled down the aisles of Congress," said Theodore R. Sizer, author of *Horace's Compromise* (1984), which argues for restructuring the traditional approach to education in American high schools *(see p. 62)*. "Some of these overstated charges did get public attention. And the public was not paying attention."[3]

Education writer George Leonard, author of *Education and Ecstasy* (1969), compared the report to a paper Sputnik. The Soviets launched that first satellite in October 1957, beating the Americans in the space race and touching off a national debate over whether American education was adequate. That in turn led to numerous changes in math and science curriculums. "A

---

[2] For background, see Paul E. Peterson, "Did the Education Commissions Say Anything?" *The Brookings Review*, winter 1983, p. 3.

[3] Persons quoted in this report were interviewed by the author unless otherwise indicated.

What Other Reports Recommend

Three recent reports not discussed in detail in the text also have made recommendations on teaching and curriculum:

Educating Americans for the 21st Century, National Science Board Commission on Precollege Education in Mathematics, Science and Technology, National Science Foundation, September 1983. States should adopt rigorous certification requirements for math, science and technology teachers, do more to recruit high-quality teachers in these areas, and adopt salary ladders to retain the best teachers. Elementary schools should require an hour of math and a half-hour of science a day, and a full year of science in grades seven and eight. College entrance requirements should be raised to four years each of math and science and one year of computer science.

Making the Grade, Task Force on Federal Elementary and Secondary Education Policy, Twentieth Century Fund, 1983. The task force advocated "master teacher" programs and proposed "reconsideration of merit-based personnel systems for teachers." Schools should strive for excellence in teaching "the basic skills of reading, writing and math; technical capability on computers; training in science and foreign languages; and knowledge of civics. . . ."

"Action for Excellence," Task Force on Education for Economic Growth, Education Commission of the States, 1983. States should "dramatically improve methods of recruiting, training and paying teachers," and create "career ladders" for teachers. School systems should establish "firm, explicit and demanding requirements concerning discipline, attendance, homework, grades and other essentials of effective schooling."

Nation at Risk" and reports by the Education Commission of the States, the Twentieth Century Fund and the National Science Foundation, among others, are playing the same role now.

Of all the recommendations in "A Nation at Risk," President Reagan appeared most enthusiastic about merit pay, which would require no federal money. He endorsed the idea in a number of speeches, putting himself in direct conflict with teachers' unions, which strongly oppose it. "There has not yet been a merit pay system that lasted any period of time that did not create more problems than it solved," declared Robert McClure, programs manager for teacher education for the National Education Association. With 1.7 million members, the NEA is the nation's largest teacher organization. The American Federation of Teachers (AFT), an AFL-CIO affiliated union of about 580,000 members, has labeled public infatuation with merit pay a "misguided preoccupation." [4]

[4] American Federation of Teachers, "Proposed Special Order of Business on Education Reform," 1983, p. 2.

Sensing an important election-year issue, Rep. Carl D. Perkins, D-Ky., chairman of the House Education and Labor Committee, appointed "an independent, bipartisan committee" to study merit pay for teachers. The committee, composed primarily of educators, held hearings last summer and concluded in a report last October that merit pay deserves cautious trials. The committee put a high priority on raises for all teachers and stricter standards for entering the profession — themes that both the NEA and AFT readily endorse. "Merit pay is but one of many pieces in a puzzle," the House study group concluded. "It can be an important piece, but it is neither inexpensive nor easy to achieve, and other pieces of the puzzle must also be put into place." [5]

In 1982, the year before the Commission on Excellence in Education called for merit pay, no state offered financial incentives to outstanding teachers.[6] Since then the legislatures of California, Florida, Tennessee and Utah and the school board of Charlotte-Mecklenburg, N.C., have instituted merit pay programs. And the Education Commission of the States reports that at least three more state legislatures have the issue under consideration. Merit pay has an almost irresistibly simple appeal: reward those who excel at their work. A Gallup Poll issued last summer indicated that 61 percent of the Americans surveyed favored paying teachers according to the quality of their work.[7] Despite the official positions of the NEA and the AFT, many teachers embrace the concept. The *American School Board Journal* expressed surprise when it reported that 62.7 percent of the teachers it surveyed in May 1983 favored merit pay.[8]

Teaching Incentives: Lessons From Past

The troublesome question is how to create a fair method for evaluating a teacher's work. Failure to answer that question has scuttled most merit pay plans in the past. The idea has been tried in hundreds of school districts since the turn of the century, but a nationwide survey conducted by the Educational Research Service (ERS) in 1978 concluded that nearly all had been abandoned.[9] The survey produced "the only data base that exists on [the history] of merit pay plans for teachers," said Glen E. Robinson, ERS president and research director.

[5] Merit Pay Task Force Report, prepared for the House Education and Labor Committee, October 1983, p. 6.
[6] Educational Research Service, "Merit Pay Plans for Teachers: Status and Descriptions," 1983, p. 59.
[7] George H. Gallup, "The 15th Annual Gallup Poll of the Public's Attitudes Toward the Public Schools," *Phi Delta Kappan*, September 1983, p. 45.
[8] Marilee C. Rist, "Our Nationwide Poll: Most Teachers Endorse the Merit Pay Concept," *The American School Board Journal*, September 1983, p. 23.
[9] ERS published the results in two reports: "Merit Pay for Teachers" (1979) and "Merit Pay Plans for Teachers" (1983).

The first recorded merit pay plan for teachers was established in Newton, Mass., in 1908. Interest in merit pay continued through the 1920s but was overtaken in the following decades by salary schedules that paid teachers on the basis of seniority. Robinson found interest revived in merit pay plans in the early 1950s, but waned over the next two decades. By the time ERS surveyed 11,502 school districts in 1978, only 115 reported using some form of merit or incentive pay. In contrast, 239 school districts said they had tried merit pay and abandoned it. By the summer of 1983, prior to enactment of new state-mandated merit pay plans, the number of active plans had dropped to 53.

Robinson hopes educators and legislators will study these unsuccessful merit pay plans to avoid their pitfalls. "With the renewed interest in paying teachers on the basis of performance as a possible means of increasing efficiency and productivity in our schools, it is important that we examine the research on merit pay and learn from those who have had experience using it," said Robinson. "It's important that we don't reinvent the wheel." [10]

Robinson found the chief cause of merit pay plan failure to be difficulty in administering teacher evaluations. Of the three assessment methods school systems reported using, teacher performance evaluation was by far the most common. It is based on the teacher's knowledge of the subjects taught, lesson planning, classroom technique, and rapport with students and staff. The problem with this kind of evaluation, Robinson found, is its lack of precision. "Research indicates that the failure of most incentive pay plans has been their inability to distinguish superior teaching results from typical teaching results in a satisfactory way by relying on performance evaluation." [11]

The second approach, evaluation of professional competence, is based primarily on academic credentials, years of experience in the classroom, and willingness to take on extra responsibilities such as serving as a mentor teacher or assisting in curriculum development. A major problem with this type of evaluation is that experience, credentials and extra duties "have not been shown to be closely related to increased student learning," said Robinson.

The third approach is based on educational productivity. Teachers are judged by how much their students learn, as determined by subject matter or skills tests. Robinson observes that schools are experienced in administering tests but loath to

[10] From Glen E. Robinson, "Paying Teachers for Performance and Productivity: Learning from Experience," ERS, May 1983.

[11] From Glen E. Robinson, "Incentive Pay for Teachers: An Analysis of Approaches," ERS, March 1984.

use them in grading teachers. One reason is that it is difficult to determine what measure of student achievement would qualify a teacher for a superior rating. On the positive side, testing offers incentives and rewards to all teachers regardless of academic credentials or years of experience.

No matter which evaluation approach is adopted, Robinson contends, school systems must be willing to implement and support a merit pay plan if it is to succeed. And the plan, he warns, should not include quotas limiting the number of teachers to be rewarded. "To rush into a hastily constructed plan without giving proper attention to a school district's state of readiness ... only increases the chances of failure and of reinforcing the belief that incentive pay for teachers is unworkable," he said.

New Experiments With Merit Pay Plans

It is too early to tell if the merit pay plans enacted in the past year will avoid the problems of their forerunners. The Utah Legislature has passed a law allocating $15.2 million for school districts to devise their own merit pay plans. California's Mentor Teacher Program gives mentor teachers $4,000 extra pay each year. In return these teachers must devote up to 40 percent of their time to developing curriculums and helping other teachers improve their skills. No more than 5 percent of certified classroom teachers in each school district may receive the pay. The Legislature set aside $10.5 million for the program in the 1983-84 school year.[12] "California is the first state that's really trying some version of merit pay," state Sen. Gary Hart, a Santa Barbara Democrat and author of the bill, said after the measure passed last July. "In a sense, it's an exciting experiment. I don't know if it's going to work, but it deserves a chance." [13]

The plan enacted by the Florida Legislature takes effect in the 1984-85 school year. The Meritorious Instructional Personnel Program creates a "career ladder" with two steps: the associate master teacher and the master teacher. To qualify for the voluntary program, teachers must pass a test covering their subject area; receive a superior performance evaluation by a three-member observation team composed of a teacher, principal and a subject-area specialist; hold a master's degree in the subject taught; have four years of teaching experience; have no unapproved absences and have tenure. Qualified teachers will receive an additional $3,000 a year for three years. After that, teachers may be tested again to renew their associate-teacher

---

[12] Other sections of the California law boost teachers' base salaries 30 percent by 1986 to $18,000, impose stricter statewide graduation requirements and offer school districts financial incentives to lenghthen the school year from 175 to 180 days. The Legislature levied $400 million in new taxes to finance the program.
[13] Quoted from *Education Week*, July 27, 1983.

Teachers' Salaries, Per Pupil Spending

Averages and rankings for public schools in each state, 1982 vs. 1972. Teachers' salaries are in thousands of dollars.

| | Teachers' Salaries | | | | Spending Per Pupil | | | |
| | Ranking | | Salary | | Ranking | | Spending | |
	'82	'72	'82	'72	'82	'72	'82	'72
Ala.	35	42	$15.4	$ 7.7	46	50	$1,835	$ 543
Alaska	1	1	29.0	14.1	1	2	5,369	1,441
Ariz.	21	14	17.4	10.1	26	22	2,305	911
Ark.	49	49	13.3	7.0	50	49	1,713	601
Calif.	10	3	19.6	11.3	22	20	2,427	932
Colo.	17	25	17.7	9.1	15	23	2,708	905
Conn.	20	15	17.4	10.1	17	7	2,683	1,110
Del.	16	11	18.0	10.2	6	8	3,125	1,097
D.C.	2	5	22.9	11.0	3	11	3,441	1,063
Fla.	32	27	15.6	9.0	27	28	2,276	861
Ga.	33	43	15.4	7.7	49	37	1,721	788
Hawaii	4	7	21.0	10.5	20	13	2,604	1,020
Idaho	37	46	15.1	7.4	44	39	1,878	732
Ill.	11	6	19.5	10.7	14	16	2,720	986
Ind.	24	19	16.9	9.6	39	34	2,008	837
Iowa	27	18	16.2	9.6	24	18	2,343	970
Kan.	36	36	15.3	8.3	29	30	2,251	854
Ky.	31	45	15.6	7.4	46	46	1,835	650
La.	39	29	14.9	8.8	40	26	2,002	867
Maine	46	31	14.0	8.8	42	36	1,985	793
Md.	12	8	19.3	10.5	7	19	2,998	962
Mass.	15	23	18.3	9.2	10	13	2,964	1,020
Mich.	3	3	21.1	11.3	19	5	2,652	1,175
Minn.	22	10	17.2	10.3	16	6	2,698	1,134
Miss.	51	50	13.0	6.5	51	48	1,685	634
Mo.	34	30	15.4	8.8	31	33	2,197	845
Mont.	28	NA	16.0	NA	13	NA	2,727	NA
Neb.	41	44	14.7	7.7	21	29	2,445	856
Nev.	18	12	17.7	10.2	35	21	2,069	917
N.H.	48	32	13.3	8.7	28	32	2,256	847
N.J.	14	20	18.3	9.5	4	4	2,385	1,219
N.M.	23	34	16.9	8.5	33	31	2,178	849
N.Y.	7	2	20.4	11.4	2	1	3,769	1,466
N.C.	29	37	15.9	8.2	36	43	2,033	695
N.D.	40	47	14.9	7.4	40	38	2,002	740
Ohio	26	26	16.2	9.1	25	25	2,321	871
Okla.	43	40	14.6	7.9	30	44	2,237	686
Ore.	13	21	18.5	9.5	5	17	3,130	979
Pa.	19	17	17.7	9.9	11	9	2,841	1,073
R.I.	9	16	19.8	10.0	9	12	2,996	1,023
S.C.	44	48	14.1	7.3	43	42	1,916	700
S.D.	47	41	13.6	7.8	37	35	2,016	796
Tenn.	45	39	14.1	8.0	48	45	1,831	659
Texas	30	35	15.7	8.4	38	46	2,012	650
Utah	25	33	16.6	8.5	45	41	1,842	707
Vt.	50	28	13.2	8.9	23	3	2,365	1,232
Va.	42	24	14.6	9.1	32	24	2,193	875
Wash.	5	13	20.7	10.2	18	27	2,679	866
W.Va.	38	38	14.9	8.0	34	40	2,173	713
Wis.	8	9	20.1	10.4	12	10	2,759	1,069
Wyo.	6	22	20.4	9.2	8	15	2,997	1,001
U.S.			17.4	9.6			2,473	934

Source: Dept. of Education, Office of Planning, Budget and Evaluation

status or apply for master-teacher status. The state Board of
Education has not yet issued rules for promotion to the master-
teacher level.

Unlike California, Florida puts no quota on the percentage of
teachers who may become associate master teachers. But the
requirement that a teacher must hold a master's degree in the
subject area taught effectively eliminates four out of every five
Florida teachers, said Jade Moore, executive director of the
Pinellas County (St. Petersburg) Classroom Teachers Association, an NEA affiliate that opposes the program.

Tennessee now has the "most comprehensive, most important and best public school improvement program in the country," said Gov. Lamar Alexander, R, when the legislature passed
his Comprehensive Educational Reform Act in mid-February.[14]
The heart of the package, which takes effect next fall, is a
five-step career ladder that will pay teachers in the top three
levels $1,000 to $7,000 a year in addition to their regular
pay. Each promotion requires the candidate to pass local evaluation.

The original proposal set quotas on the number of teachers
who could qualify for the top two levels. The ceilings were
removed after opposition from the Tennessee Education Association, an NEA affiliate, stalled action on the measure in 1983.
"The limit now will be the (evaluation) standards," said John
Parish, the governor's press secretary. "If the standards are set
high enough, you won't have any problem."

No less bold, but on a smaller scale, is the merit pay plan
approved last December by the Charlotte-Mecklenburg, N.C.,
school system. The plan, which takes effect next fall, has six
steps: two years of probation, one or two years as a career
teacher nominee, two years as a career teacher candidate, then
three career-status levels. Tenure comes with promotion to Career Level I, which will take five to six years. Those who fail to
obtain tenure will be asked to leave the system. Those who
make the grade will be rewarded far beyond current salary
levels, which range between $13,900 and $24,900. Career Level I
teachers could earn the equivalent today of $34,000, Career
Level II $35,500 and Career Level III $37,000. Each step would
entail additional duties, such as serving as mentor teachers,
trouble-shooting with problem schools or working with curriculum development.

---

[14] The Comprehensive Education Reform Act of 1984 will pump $1 billion in additional
money into Tennessee public schools over the next three years. The money will come from a
1-cent increase in the state's sales tax to 5.5 cents. The program gave all teachers a 10
percent salary hike, lengthened the school year from 175 to 180 days and raised entrance
requirements to teacher education programs.

The plan got mixed reviews from the local teachers' unions. "I'm very excited and very pleased about it," said Olin Flowe, president of the AFT's Charlotte chapter. Keith Howey, president of the NEA's affiliate in Charlotte, said his teachers "are split 50-50 over the program." School Superintendent Jay Robinson, who designed the program, called it "a significant risk," but for a worthy purpose. He said it is intended to remove the possibility that a student will be assigned to a mediocre or poor teacher. "This plan, if properly implemented in the long run, will ensure that all teachers are outstanding," said Robinson.[15]

Testing the Teachers

CRITICISM OF TEACHERS and college programs that train them has paralleled the rapid growth of the profession from the early years of this century. A classic study of Pennsylvania teacher education students conducted between 1928-32 found that prospective teachers scored below the average of all college seniors taking standardized tests. The report speculated that the results would be similar in other states. "One tends to conclude," declared the authors of the report, "that [teachers] have inferior minds." [16]

Later studies produced similar results. The 1951-53 Selective Service College Qualification tests found that prospective education majors consistently scored lowest of any group. James D. Koerner conducted an extensive survey of teacher education programs at 63 colleges and universities in the early 1960s. "By about any academic standard that can be applied," he wrote in his book *The Miseducation of American Teachers*, "students in teacher-training programs are among the least able on the campus. . . ." The teacher education faculty fared no better under Koerner's scrutiny: "It is an indecorous thing to say and obviously offensive to most educationists, but it is the truth and it should be said: the inferior intellectual quality of the education faculty is *the* fundamental limitation of the field, and will remain so, in my judgment, for some time to come." [17]

Koerner's book sparked widespread demands for change. That almost nothing did is attributable more to timing than to indifference. School populations grew to new highs each year in

[15] Quoted from *The Charlotte Observer*, Dec. 14, 1983.
[16] From James D. Koerner, *The Miseducation of American Teachers*, 1963, p. 40.
[17] *Ibid.*, p. 39.

the 1960s with the postwar baby-boom generation. Teachers were in short supply and schools welcomed fresh recruits with open arms. The decade also marked a turbulent period for public schools; racial integration, remedial and compensatory programs, education of the handicapped, anti-Vietnam War protests and a shift toward "relevant" curriculums all diverted attention from teacher training.

The latest wave of criticism may leave more lasting results because of demographic shifts now under way. Public school enrollment peaked in 1971 at 51.3 million and has been on a continuous slide ever since. Except in math and science, there is now a teacher glut, and fewer people are entering the profession. Between 1966 and 1982, the percentage of college freshmen, male and female, interested in becoming teachers dropped from 21.7 percent to 4.7 percent.[18] But the glut may soon turn to a shortage.

The current teaching force is "graying" and retiring at a rapid rate. Approximately half of the nation's 2.1 million public school teachers will be replaced by 1991, according to the National Center for Educational Statistics. And children of the baby-boom generation are expected to reverse the 13-year enrollment decline beginning next fall, causing a 12 to 18 percent enrollment increase by the year 2000. Demand for teachers again will rise. Schools are expected to hire 1.3 million new teachers by 1990. Denis P. Doyle, director of education policy studies at the American Enterprise Institute in Washington, D.C., finds in these figures a "rare demographic opportunity to overhaul the teacher force." He sees "a window of opportunity . . . to alter for decades the quality of public school instruction." [19]

Setting Stricter Certification Standards

Many states already have taken steps to improve the quality of their teachers. Twenty-five states now require prospective teachers to pass a proficiency test before receiving certification. Louisiana's teacher competency testing law, enacted in 1977, served as a model for other states. It declared that "any person applying for initial certification as a teacher must have satisfactorily passed an examination to include English proficiency, pedagogical knowledge, and knowledge of his area of specialization." More recently, 17 states have acted to keep academically weak teacher education candidates from entering teacher training programs. Students in these states must pass basic skills tests before taking teacher training classes.

---

[18] From Denis P. Doyle, "Window of Opportunity," *The Wilson Quarterly*, New Year's 1984, p. 97.
[19] *Ibid.*, p. 98.

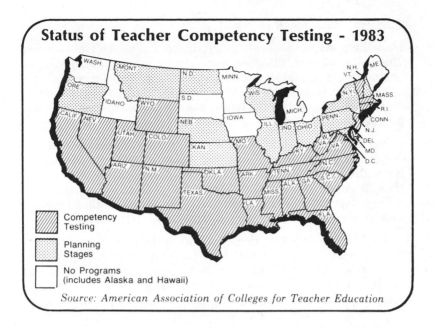

Status of Teacher Competency Testing - 1983

Competency
Testing

Planning
Stages

No Programs
(includes Alaska and Hawaii)

Source: American Association of Colleges for Teacher Education

The new emphasis on testing prospective teachers is a response to concern about the quality of those choosing teaching as a career. "Never before in U.S. history has the caliber of those entering the teaching profession been as low as it is today," declared a study published in 1983.[20] The study found that women, who traditionally provided most of the nation's public school teachers, now have more career choices. Many of "the best and brightest" who once would have become teachers are opting for higher-paying professions such as law, medicine and business. As a result, the 1982 Scholastic Aptitude Test scores for college-bound seniors heading for education degrees were 81 points below the national average in math and verbal skills, a combined score of 813 out of a possible 1,600 points.[21]

The drive to upgrade teacher qualifications is picking up steam. The number of states with teacher competency programs of any kind rose from three in 1977 to 12 in 1980 and 30 in 1983, according to J. T. Sandefur, dean of the College of Education at Western Kentucky University *(see map above)*. Sandefur, who surveyed states in October 1983, found 12 more states studying or planning for some form of teacher competency testing.[22]

The two major teachers' unions support state plans to tighten requirements for teacher education and entry into the profession. AFT policy states that, "All beginning teachers should be tested and required to meet a standard which represents at

[20] "The American Teacher," Feistritzer Publications, 1983, p. 59.
[21] For background, see "Illiteracy in America," *E.R.R.*, 1983 Vol. I, pp. 475-490.
[22] Figures from J. T. Sandefur, "State Assessment Trends," *American Association of Colleges for Teacher Education Briefs*, March 1984, p. 17.

least the average of all college graduates." The AFT also favors "higher teacher certification requirements that specifically include greater emphasis on subject matter competence and less emphasis on [teaching] methods courses." NEA policy supports "increasing the academic requirements for admission into and graduation from schools of education." [23]

Increased interest in teacher testing raises a number of important issues about the use and abuse of tests. In his survey Sandefur found that most states use standardized tests rather than developing their own. "Apparently, this is a result of the prohibitive costs of test development and the additional advantage of national and state comparability," he said.[24]

The nation's leading developer of standardized tests is the Educational Testing Service, based in Princeton, N.J. The company is best known for the Scholastic Aptitude Test, but it also produces the NTE, formerly known as the National Teacher Examinations, now used by 12 states for teacher certification.[25] The NTE is designed to measure academic preparation — not teaching ability. "Interest in teacher testing has been very intense in the last several years, primarily as a method for teacher certification," said Ed Masonis, NTE program administrator.

A recent addition to the NTE is the Pre-Professional Skills Test intended to screen academically poor students out of teacher education programs. Introduced in 1983, it tests basic proficiency in reading, writing and math. Texas and Kansas are the first two states to require the test for admission into schools of education; several others are considering it.

The testing service also permits NTE use in establishing who deserves merit or incentive pay, provided the plans are voluntary and the test is not used as a sole criterion for advancement. Because its program is voluntary, Florida may use NTE area exams as one criterion in promoting teachers to associate master teacher status. "People don't lose jobs and they don't lose any money (if they don't make a passing score)," said Masonis of ETS.

Controversies Over Competency Testing

ETS strenuously objects, however, to use of the NTE as the sole device to weed out inferior teachers already in the classroom. "The NTE does not measure things like how well a teacher can set expectations or relate to students," said Gregory R. Anrig, president of the testing service. "Using it as the sole criterion for determining employment or pay scales violates all

[23] "Resolutions, Legislative Program and New Business, 1983-84" NEA, 1983, p. 33.
[24] Sandefur, *op. cit.*, p. 18.
[25] Arkansas, California, Delaware, Louisiana, Mississippi, New Mexico, New York, North Carolina, South Carolina, Tennessee, Virginia and West Virginia.

kinds of federal laws about the relevance of tests to the work-place. The members of no other profession are required to pass standardized tests in order to maintain their jobs." [26]

ETS adopted this policy last November shortly after the Arkansas Legislature passed a law requiring teachers to pass a portion of the NTE or lose their jobs. The Houston, Texas, Independent School District already had adopted a similar requirement. Arkansas Gov. Bill Clinton, D, a former Rhodes Scholar, promised Arkansas parents he would weed out incompetent teachers if they would foot the bill for better schools through a 1-cent sales tax increase. [27] Following the ETS policy announcement, Clinton vowed to find another test to carry out his program.

Whatever test Arkansas uses is bound to be unpopular with teachers. An NEA investigative committee studied the impact of the testing law and concluded in March that it already had weakened classroom discipline by putting teachers on the defensive with their students, alienated teachers and drained money from "positive educational reforms." "The testing law is a mistake," the report declared. "We call on all parties involved to scrap or amend this counterproductive measure."

Critics of teacher testing point out that subject mastery is not in itself a guarantee of teacher competence. Other factors such as commitment to the profession and rapport with students influence a teacher's ability to impart knowledge. Testing for basic competence also does nothing to ensure that teachers can go beyond the basics. In a comprehensive survey of what goes on inside classrooms, John I. Goodlad, former dean of the Graduate School of Education at the University of California at Los Angeles, found:

> "Developing 'the ability to read, write, and handle basic arithmetical operations,' as the states' educational documents put it, pervades instruction from the first through the ninth grades, and the lower tracks of courses beyond. What the schools in our sample did not appear to be doing in these subjects was developing all the qualities commonly listed under 'intellectual development': the ability to think rationally, the ability to use, evaluate, and accumulate knowledge, a desire for further learning. Only *rarely* did we find evidence to suggest instruction likely to go much beyond mere possession of information to a level of understanding its implications and either applying it or exploring its possible applications." [28]

---

[26] Quoted from *The New York Times*, Nov. 29, 1983.
[27] The Arkansas Legislature also lengthened the school day from 5 to 5½ hours, raised the dropout age from 16 to 17, tripled spending for vocational education, established basic skills testing for third, sixth and eighth graders and raised teachers salaries.
[28] John I. Goodlad, *A Place Called School*, 1984, p. 236.

Changing the System

FEW WHO CRITICIZE the public schools blame the system; most fault teachers for poor results. But the authors of three recent studies believe the system bears scrutiny and could use more than just tinkering with longer days and tougher gradua- tion and teacher education requirements. Theodore R. Sizer, author of *Horace's Compromise*, calls the emphasis on tighten- ing teacher education requirements misguided. "Until you change the working conditions for teachers, schools of education are going to have a great deal of difficulty in attracting able students," Sizer said.

Ernest L. Boyer, president of the Carnegie Foundation for the Advancement of Teaching, concurs. In his book *High School*, Boyer urges three basic changes in the way teachers use their time: no more than four formal classes a day (down from five or six), a minimum of 60 minutes each day for class preparation, and an end to hall or lunchroom monitoring duty. "Improving working conditions is, we believe, at the center of our effort to improve teaching," said Boyer, a former U.S. commissioner of education.[29] More of the same simply isn't good enough, warns Goodlad in *A Place Called School*. The push to require students to take more English, math, science and history courses and to spend more time in class could lead to making schools "more boring, less fun, more repetitious, [with] still fewer encounters with significant intellectual problems. ..." Goodlad wrote.[30] Goodlad coordinated the work of 43 researchers who over eight years studied 38 schools in 13 communities across the country. "American schools are in trouble," he concluded. "In fact, the problems of schooling are of such crippling proportions that many schools may not survive. It is possible that our entire public education system is nearing collapse."[31]

Goodlad's researchers found that students became less and less involved in education as they advanced through the grades. Typical primary teachers use several techniques to teach a subject like arithmetic, from chalkboard explanations to games and drawing. But typical high school teachers spend nearly all of their time lecturing and monitoring seat work. Consequently, students in the upper grades suffer from too much "teacher talk," Goodlad said. "The average instructional day in junior or senior high includes 150 minutes of talking. Of this, only seven minutes is generated by students."[32] Teachers resort to fact-

[29] Ernest L. Boyer, *High School, A Report on Secondary Education in America*, 1983, p. 161.
[30] Goodlad, *op. cit.*
[31] *Ibid.*, p. 1.
[32] Quoted from *The New York Times*, July 19, 1983.

Student Performance

The following table shows rankings by state based on scores recorded by high school seniors on college entrance examinations in 1982. States are listed in one of two columns depending on which test was taken by a majority of the college-bound students in each state. Washington state performance scores are not included because fewer than 20 percent of the state's high school seniors took either test. In case of ties, average rank is used.

American College Test (ACT) 1982 Rankings for 28 States		Scholastic Aptitude Test (SAT) 1982 Rankings for 22 States	
1	Wisconsin	1	New Hampshire
2	Iowa	2	Oregon
3	Minnesota	3	Vermont
4	Nebraska	4	California
5	Colorado	5	Delaware
6	Montana	6.5	New York
7	Wyoming	6.5	Connecticut
8	South Dakota	8	Maine
9	Ohio	9.5	Florida
10.5	Kansas	9.5	Maryland
10.5	Idaho	11.5	Massachusetts
13.5	Arizona	11.5	Virginia
13.5	Alaska	13	Pennsylvania
13.5	Michigan	14	Rhode Island
13.5	Missouri	15	New Jersey
16	Illinois	16	Texas
17	Utah	17	Indiana
18	Nevada	18	Hawaii
19	North Dakota	19	North Carolina
20	Arkansas	20	Georgia
21.5	New Mexico	21	District of Columbia
21.5	Oklahoma	22	South Carolina
23.5	Kentucky		
23.5	Tennessee		
25	West Virginia		
26	Alabama		
27	Louisiana		
28	Mississippi		

Source: Department of Education, Office of Planning, Budget and Evaluation

oriented lecturing because they do not know how to teach for higher levels of learning," Goodlad contends. To correct this deficiency, he proposes a two-year program of professional studies and classroom experience to teach teachers methods that would challenge students to use their minds more actively. "This nation cannot continue to afford the brief, casual, conforming preparation now experienced by those who will staff its classrooms." [33]

[33] Goodlad, *op. cit.*, p. 316.

Goodlad has what may strike many as a surprising recommendation concerning ability grouping of high school students. Grouping is the practice of putting students into fast-, medium- or slow-moving sections of required subjects such as English and history. The assumption is that when students are put into mixed groups, class work sinks to the lowest common denominator. Goodlad's research suggests that assumption is wrong. He found that students in middle and low groups got shortchanged academically, while students in mixed classes were treated more like those in academically challenging, high-group classes. Furthermore, teacher expectations were higher for students in high-group and mixed classes, as indicated by increased levels of homework.

New Core Curriculum for High Schools

Boyer also challenges some of the prevailing assumptions about the way high schools are run. He recommends a new high school curriculum for all students, which would require three and one-half years of history and civics, three years of English, and two each of math, science and foreign language. The curriculum also would require a semester study of the arts, a semester study of career options and a semester-long senior independent study program.

Boyer would do away with the practice of tracking students into college-preparatory, vocational and general studies. The three-track system "should be replaced by a single-track program — one that provides a core education for all students plus a pattern of electives, keeping options open for both work and further education," Boyer said.[34] Drawing on Goodlad's research on vocational programs, Boyer argues that schools are giving job training at the expense of basic education. The students hurt most by this are minorities, especially blacks and Hispanics. He cites recent studies that report no difference in employment potential between male graduates of vocational programs and male graduates of general education programs. Given the increasing complexity and higher intellectual skill demands of the job market, "it appears that high school vocational programs [in the future] will be either irrelevant or inadequate." [35]

Novel Approach to Schools: Less is More

Sizer, too, would restructure the high school curriculum, but by limiting what is offered, not expanding what is required. "There are limited resources and limited time. And we keep piling more obligations on the schools," he said. "We expect

[34] Boyer, *op. cit.*, p. 126.
[35] *Ibid.*, p. 123.

them to teach kids how to use their minds well, how to grow up, how to relate to their parents and to their society, how to prepare for a job. We give them drug education, nuclear education, driver's education, every kind of conceivable thing — each one of which can be defended on its own merits. But there isn't enough time to do them all." Sizer proposes less diversity in the curriculum, less laxity in demanding student mastery of basics, and less control by state and local governments.

Sizer would trim the curriculum to four basic areas: inquiry and expression [primarily writing], math and science, literature and the arts, philosophy and history. Only students who passed minimum competency tests would be allowed to enroll in high schools. Those who did not pass would enroll in intensive basic skills courses. Once in high school, students could advance at their own pace to fulfill graduation requirements. Every student would be enrolled in each curriculum area all the time, and teachers would have no more than 80 students a day. Teachers would do far less talking and much more "coaching" of individual students. "When it comes to learning how to solve a problem, being lectured doesn't help very much. We learn by the experience of having someone criticize our work," the essence of teacher coaching, Sizer said. Like Boyer, Sizer would do away with tracking and ability grouping. Vocational education also would go. "The most important vocational education in a rapidly changing economy is the flexibility that comes from knowing how to think clearly," Sizer said.

Unlike the authors of other education studies, Sizer plans to put his ideas to work. From his new post as dean of the Brown University School of Education, he will oversee long-term projects in five or more schools willing to implement his recommendations. He hopes to start with one or two schools in the fall.

Some critics have accused Sizer of developing elitist recommendations designed to meet the needs of the brightest and most highly motivated students like those he used to teach at Harvard University and Phillips Academy, an exclusive college preparatory school. He readily admits he does not know whether his ideas will work for all students. But he is optimistic. "There are people with substantial experience in different kinds of settings who think that the general principles we are pushing square with their experience," Sizer said. "One important aspect of our work is that we don't have a model to plug in. And in taking that position, I find lots of colleagues out there in schools across the country respond very positively. It is about time someone figured out that there isn't one best way of doing things."

Selected Bibliography

Books

Conant, James Bryant, *The Education of American Teachers*, McGraw-Hill, 1963.

Boyer, Ernest L., *High School, A Report on Secondary Education in America*, Harper & Row, 1983.

Goodlad, John I., *A Place Called School*, McGraw-Hill, 1984.

Koerner, James D., *The Miseducation of American Teachers*, Houghton Mifflin Co., 1963.

Lipsitz, Joan, *Successful Schools for Young Adolescents*, Transaction Books, 1984.

Ravitch, Diane, *The Troubled Crusade, American Education 1945-1980*, Basic Books, 1983.

Sizer, Theodore R., *Horace's Compromise: The Dilemma of the American High School*, Houghton Mifflin Co., 1984.

Articles

Doyle, Denis P., "Window of Opportunity," *The Wilson Quarterly*, New Year's 1984.

Gallup, George H., "The 15th Annual Gallup Poll of the Public's Attitudes Toward the Public Schools," *Phi Delta Kappan*, September 1983.

Leonard, George, "The Great School Reform Hoax," *Esquire*, April 1984.

Sandefur, J. T., "State Assessment Trends," *American Association of Colleges for Teacher Education Briefs*, March 1984.

Rist, Marilee C., "Our Nationwide Poll: Most Teachers Endorse the Merit Pay Concept," *The American School Board Journal*, September 1983.

Peterson, Paul E., "Did the Education Commissions Say Anything?" *The Brookings Review*, winter 1983.

Reports and Studies

Editorial Research Reports, "Competency Tests," 1978 Vol. II, p. 603; "Illiteracy in America," 1983 Vol. I, p. 475; "Post-Sputnik Education," 1982 Vol. II, p. 653.

Educational Research Service, "Evaluating Teacher Performance," 1978.

——"Merit Pay Plans for Teachers: Status and Descriptions, 1983.

National Commission on Excellence in Education, "A Nation at Risk: The Imperative for Educational Reform," April 1983.

Robinson, Glen E., "Incentive Pay for Teachers: An Analysis of Approaches," Educational Research Service, March 1984.

——"Paying Teachers for Performance and Productivity: Learning from Experience," Educational Research Service, May 1983.

Graphics: Cover art by George Rebh; p. 57 map by Staff Artist Belle Burkhart.

POST-SPUTNIK EDUCATION

by

Jean Rosenblatt

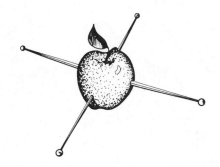

Sept. 3
1 9 8 2

POST-SPUTNIK EDUCATION

THE Soviet Union's launching of Sputnik 25 years ago, on Oct. 4, 1957, sent the American education establishment into a tailspin. At least since the early 1940s the trend in education had been toward the social development of children rather than an emphasis on hard academic subject matter. At the same time, however, there had been a growing concern about whether math and science education was adequate and whether enough students were prepared and interested in seeking careers that would help advance American technology.

Russia's dramatic exploit in space[1] highlighted the costs of neglecting rigorous academic training, particularly in math and science, and galvanized this nation to action. President Eisenhower stressed the importance of education to national security, and American leaders rushed to bolster the nation's science, math and foreign language instruction, funding university research and development projects, providing scholarships and otherwise encouraging young people to enter technological careers. This was done largely through the National Defense Education Act of 1958, which was in many ways the forerunner of general federal aid to education (see p. 73).

Twenty-five years later educators, scientists, industrialists and other concerned citizens are again declaring that American children are not being adequately educated, which they see as posing a threat to economic growth and national security. Last spring President Reagan told a meeting sponsored by the National Academy of Sciences that problems in math and science teaching are "serious enough to compromise the nation's future ability to develop and advance our traditional industrial base to compete in international marketplaces."[2] Dr. Harry Lustig, dean of science at City College of New York, said, "I see us becoming industrially a second-rate power."

Declining student competency, reduced requirements for graduation, a shortage of qualified teachers and an inadequate

---

[1] Sputnik I was the first space satellite to be put into orbit around the Earth. This small (184-pound) unmanned sphere circled the globe every 96.2 minutes. A month later, on Nov. 3, a bigger Sputnik II (1,120 pounds) was sent aloft carrying a dog into orbit. The United States ultimately captured the greatest glory in the space race by sending men to the moon for the first time in 1969.

[2] Written statement presented to the meeting, the national Convocation on Preschool Education in Mathematics and Science. It was held in Washington, D.C., May 12, 1982.

supply of instructional materials are factors cited as evidence of
the poor state of math and science instruction, at a time when
America's competitors as well as allies are placing greater emphasis on these subjects *(see p. 71)*. Experts say a scarcity of
trained personnel in various scientific fields is cause for alarm.
They add that the pool from which such personnel can be drawn
is diminishing, even as the need is increasing. At the same time,
by luring math and science teachers into industry with high
salaries, "we are consuming our seed corn," said Denis P. Doyle,
director of education policy studies at the American Enterprise
Institute in Washington, D.C.[3]

An overall decline in the public's scientific literacy is also
perceived. "Even now too few Americans have the science or
mathematics grounding to keep America in the forefront technologically and economically, and it appears that our future
citizenry as a whole will be even *less* well prepared to understand and support scientific development," say the authors of a
recent report published by the American Association for the
Advancement of Science (AAAS).[4]

These concerns are surfacing at a time when the federal
government is slashing funding for elementary and secondary
education, including science education, and individual states,
under their own budgetary strains, are reducing their support as
well. Many people advocate a "Sputnik-style" federal investment, but the Reagan administration opposes such an effort.
"We disagree with those who say that the federal government
should be ultimately responsible for this problem," presidential
policy adviser Edwin L. Harper told the National Academy of
Sciences meeting. Businesses, the states and local school districts must play their part, he added. Wherever the solution lies,
educational historian Diane Ravitch told Editorial Research
Reports, "now it's almost as though we're waiting for a Sputnik
to focus everyone's attention on the problem."

Evidence of Crisis in Math and Science

One of the first signs of trouble educators point to is the
steady decline of achievement test scores in math and science
over the last 15 years *(see box, p. 69)*. The most drastic drops
have occurred in the higher grades. The decline is taking place
mostly among youngsters not planning careers in science or
engineering. Education analysts say that means the most advanced students are learning as much as they ever did but the
majority of students are learning less. The Advisory Panel on
the SAT Score Decline has explained that the downward trend
between 1963 and 1970 could be accounted for by changes in the

---

[3] Writing in *The Washington Post*, March 10, 1982.
[4] "Education in the Sciences: A Developing Crisis," 1982, p. 3.

Declining Math Test Scores

School Year	SAT Averages*	School Year	SAT Averages*
1966-67	495	1974-75	473
1967-68	494	1975-76	470
1968-69	491	1976-77	471
1969-70	488	1977-78	469
1970-71	487	1978-79	466
1971-72	482	1979-80	466
1972-73	481	1980-81	466
1973-74	478		

*Scholastic Aptitude Test scale ranges from 200 to 800.

Source: Educational Testing Service, Princeton, N.J.

test-taking group; during that period it included more college-bound minority and low-income students than before.[5] But since 1970 the composition of test-takers has remained fairly stable, and scores have dropped even more sharply.

In trying to explain the decline the panel concluded that aside from the usual villains of high divorce rates, television, Vietnam, Watergate and drugs, lower academic standards may also have played a large part. "Absenteeism formerly considered intolerable is now condoned," said the AAAS report. "An 'A' or 'B' means a good deal less than it used to. Promotion from one grade to another has become almost automatic. Homework has apparently been cut about in half." According to a recent study by the National Research Council, only a third of the nation's high schools offer more than one year of math or science and at least half of all high-school seniors graduated without a single year of physics or chemistry.[6] A sample survey found that over 56 percent of the high schools require no math courses or only one for graduation.[7]

With requirements for graduation reduced, children are evidently passing through the system without acquiring basic skills. This has led to the so-called back-to-basics movement, which some observers say often has had the effect of reducing learning to its lowest level at the expense of a more rounded education. The National Congress of Parents and Teachers noted: "Though emphasis on acquiring basic skills is at the heart of the education process, there is a distinct possibility of basics becoming *the* curriculum rather than just *part* of the curriculum. Another problem, with an overemphasis on basics,

[5] College Entrance Examination Board. "On Further Examination," report of the Advisory Panel on the Scholastic Aptitude Test, 1977.
[6] Cited by Otto Sturzenegger in "We'd Better Do Something About Science Education," *Industry Week*, July 26, 1982.
[7] Catherine P. Ailes and Francis R. Rushing, *The Science Race: Training and Utilization of Scientists and Engineers, US and USSR*, Crane Russak, 1982.

is a tendency to teach children only those things for which they will be tested, a tendency that leads to mediocrity." [8]

According to the authors of the 1980 National Science Foundation and Department of Education study, "Science and Engineering Education for the 1980s and Beyond," the focus on basics is affecting science teaching, particularly in elementary schools. Since science is not considered basic at this level, the authors say, what little attention has been paid it is diminishing.

In addition to test scores, enrollments in upper-level science and math classes have also declined over the years. In 1960-61, for example, 59 percent of all students in grades 9-12 were enrolled in at least one science class. By 1976-77 only 48 percent were. The National Science Foundation concluded that about one-sixth of all high-school graduates have taken junior- and senior-level science and math courses. Half of the graduates have taken no science or math beyond the 10th grade and only half of those entering college have had any significant exposure to physical science or advanced math beyond the 10th grade.

It has been suggested that lower enrollments and declining achievements may be related to the fact that many colleges and universities have reduced their standards for admission to attract more students. The Carnegie Council on Policy Studies in Higher Education concluded that reduced college entrance and retention requirements have harmed high-school academic standards.

Industry's Lure to Qualified Teachers

A related cause for alarm is a shortage of qualified teachers, particularly in physics, chemistry and math. According to the National Science Teachers Association (NSTA), between 1971 and 1980 there was a 77 percent decline in the number of teachers qualified to teach math and a 65 percent decline in the number qualified to teach science in secondary schools. The percentage of those trained to teach math and science who actually do so has also declined. The combined effect, says NSTA, is a 68 percent reduction in newly employed science teachers and an 80 percent reduction of math teachers since 1971.

Another survey by the same association found that among newly employed science and math teachers, about half were unqualified to teach those subjects. They had been employed on an emergency basis because no qualified teachers could be found. Shortages were especially apparent in states where high-

---

[8] Quoted in "Science and Engineering Education for the 1980s and Beyond," National Science Foundation and the Department of Education, 1980, p. 48.

technology industries are numerous, providing abundant job opportunities to persons trained in math and science. Computerization in industry has been a boon, especially to persons trained in math. Until the age of computers, their job market was relatively small. Experts have estimated that schools are losing five times as many science and math teachers to industry as to retirement.

Teacher shortages in math and science not only result from better-paying work in industry but also, evidently, from disillusionment with teaching. The conditions under which teachers work, including low pay and a general indifference to their status, have deteriorated because of rising costs, taxpayer resistance to higher teaching salaries, and lack of student motivation. The financial factors along with declining enrollments have particularly affected math and science education because they have led to less spending for equipment and facilities needed to teach those subjects.

One form of teacher support that grew out of post-Sputnik federal involvement was summer institutes funded by the National Science Foundation. But their funding started declining in 1968, all but disappeared in 1975 and was eliminated altogether this year. Research on the summer institute program concluded that it did have a significant impact on secondary school science and math education but that few of the least qualified teachers participated.[9]

How U.S. Compares With Other Nations

In "Science and Engineering Education for the 1980s and Beyond," the authors wrote: "The declining emphasis on science and mathematics in our school systems is in marked contrast to other industrialized countries. Japan, Germany, and the Soviet Union all provide rigorous training in science and mathematics for nearly all their students at the pre-college levels. We fear a loss of our competitive edge." In these countries, unlike the United States, national policy promotes comprehensive science and math education for everyone, not just those planning to specialize.

In the U.S.S.R. and Japan, for example, a large number of people in both government and industry have engineering degrees. In Japan, more engineering degrees have been granted in recent years than in the United States, which has nearly twice as many people. About 20 percent of all baccalaureate degrees and 40 percent of all master's degrees are in engineering, compared to about 5 percent at both levels in the United States.

---

[9] Stanley Helgeson, "Impact of the National Science Foundation Summer Institute Program," The Ohio State University, 1974.

Japanese educators explain that in Japan engineering degrees are seen as a ticket to success in much the same way M.B.A. — master of business administration — degrees have been regarded here.

Unlike the United States, secondary education in Japan is weighted heavily toward science and math. A national guideline calls for 25 percent of class time in grades seven through nine to be spent in those studies. In grades nine through twelve nearly all college-bound students take three natural science courses and four math courses. Only 34 percent of the approximately three million U.S. high-school students complete three years of math by the time they graduate, according to Paul DeHart Hurd, professor emeritus at Stanford University.[10]

Science instruction begins early for the college-bound in Germany. By the time the German student reaches the fifth grade, he or she is spending two to three hours a week on each of four science-math courses — biology, chemistry, geometry and physics. In the United States, out of a 25-hour school week, elementary students receive about one hour of instruction in science and four in math. Most don't study algebra until the ninth grade; in Germany it is introduced in the seventh grade.

Science and math reportedly receive more attention in the Soviet Union than in any other country. Math is introduced in the first grade, biology in the fifth, physics in the sixth and chemistry in the seventh. Algebra and geometry are taught in the sixth and seventh grades, and trigonometry in grades eight through 10. Only 5 percent of the high-school students in California, for example, take trigonometry at all, according to Michael W. Kirst, an education professor at Stanford University.

About 500,000 Americans take calculus in the 12th grade or first year of college, while it is part of the Soviet high-school curriculum for more than five million students. In a recently prepared survey of curriculum materials in the Soviet Union, the author concluded that secondary-level Soviet math and science courses are comparable to introductory college courses in the United States. His survey also indicated that Russian science and math teachers were more numerous and better prepared than their American counterparts.[11]

---

[10] Writing in *The Washington Post*, May 16, 1982.
[11] Nicholas DeWitt, "Current Status and Determinants of Science Education in Soviet Secondary Schools," prepared for the National Academy of Sciences, 1980.

Education Trends Since 1957

S PUTNIK came at a time when if it hadn't happened it would have had to have been invented," said Diane Ravitch in a recent interview. "It gave a push to a lot of nascent trends." One of these trends was increased federal support for science and engineering education. At the end of World War II, President Roosevelt asked Vannevar Bush, the director of the Office of Scientific Research and Development, to examine science research in the United States. One aspect of Bush's inquiry was the adequacy of education in discovering and developing scientific talent. Bush's report, "Science — The Endless Frontier," for the first time established this development as a federal responsibility.[12]

The National Science Foundation, established in 1950, was the government's primary means for doing this, but it concentrated on graduate students who had already chosen science and engineering careers. In the mid-1950s, however, it began paying attention to elementary and secondary education through teacher training institutes and curriculum development. After Sputnik was launched the foundation's budget for science education increased substantially; Americans who examined the Soviet education system for clues to Russian superiority in space discovered the Soviet emphasis on science, mathematics and foreign languages.[13] Congress than passed the National Defense Education Act (NDEA) in 1958 to support the study of these subjects in American schools.

The act accounted for a major increase in federal spending on elementary and secondary education.[14] The stated aim was to "meet the present education emergency" by providing federal financial assistance to individuals and states "in order to insure trained manpower of sufficient quality and quantity to meet the national defense needs." One of its provisions was for new science education programs in the U.S. Office (now Department) of Education. The potential overlap between the Office of Education and the National Science Foundation, with its new authority to support science, engineering and math education at all levels, was resolved through the understanding that the Office of Education would operate mainly through the states and local school systems and the NSF would operate through

---

[12] Vannevar Bush, "Science — The Endless Frontier," first issued in 1945, reprinted by the National Science Foundation, 1980.

[13] America also encountered great difficulties in its attempt to improve student proficiency in foreign languages. See "Foreign Languages: Tongue-Tied Americans," *E.R.R.*, 1980 Vol. II, pp. 677-696. The post-Sputnik era is reviewed in pp. 687-689.

[14] This funding rose from $128.3 billion in fiscal year 1957 to $224.9 billion in 1960.

colleges and universities, individual scientists and scientific societies.

Between 1959 and 1962 three government reports on science and engineering education recommended an expanded federal role in those areas.[15] NSF funding, however, has been declining since the late 1950s *(see graph)* and, according to Sarah E. Klein, president of the National Science Teachers Association, "the present cluster of national problems in secondary school science and math education can in large part be attributed to the National Science Foundation's negligence of . . . their [sic] congressionally mandated mission." [16]

Focus on Gifted; Increased Federal Aid

Changes in the teaching of physics, chemistry, biology and math over the past 25 years have largely resulted from NSF curriculum development efforts. When these were implemented in the late 1950s and early 1960s, students were encouraged to discover the sciences by experimenting rather than by memorizing formulas and theorems. Mathematicians began to question the traditional curriculum and to search for better ways of teaching math. From their efforts came the "new" math. It sought to broaden the understanding of mathematics among students by introducing them to the fundamental principles and theories. "Conceptual insight" became a favorite phrase. Students were introduced to set theory, the concepts of union and intersection, and the associative, distributive and commutative laws. They were also taught how to compute in base systems other than base 10.

These efforts were largely directed toward gifted children, as the "pursuit of excellence" became a rallying cry for American educators during this period. A national conference on the academically talented secondary school student, sponsored by the National Education Association, met in Washington in February 1958 and, under the chairmanship of James B. Conant, president emeritus of Harvard, drew up a number of recommendations for activating gifted-child programs in the public schools. During this period the number of research projects on the nature of giftedness increased significantly. "Probably 20 times as much material was published on this subject in the decade 1950-1960 as in any previous 10-year period," Gertrude H. Hildreth wrote in *Introduction to the Gifted* (1966).

Changes in social studies education also began to take place. In the mid-1950s history and geography dominated social stud-

15 "Education for the Age of Science," 1959; "Scientific Progress, The Universities and the Federal Government," 1960; and "Meeting Manpower Needs in Science and Technology," 1962. All reports were prepared by the President's Science Advisory Committee.
16 Testimony before the Subcommittee on HUD-Independent Agencies of the House Appropriations Committee, May 18, 1982.

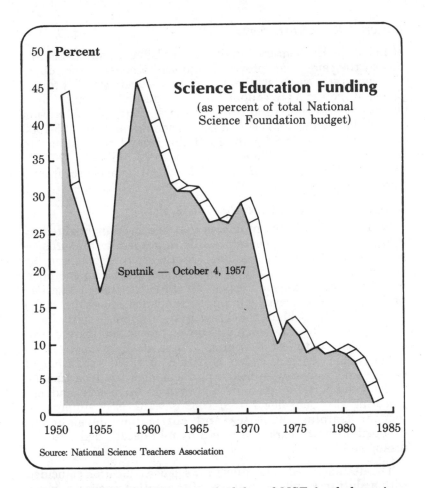

Science Education Funding

(as percent of total National Science Foundation budget)

Sputnik — October 4, 1957

Source: National Science Teachers Association

ies but by the early 1960s a much-debated NSF-funded curriculum called "Man: A Course of Study" had been introduced, designed for children in the fifth and sixth grades. Writing in the April 1979 issue of *Educational Leadership,* education Professor Gerald Ponder said, "The social studies curriculum was to become organized by the concepts and principles that formed the structure of the scientific disciplines instead of the chronological organization of history. Rather than memorizing names and dates, students were to inquire into causality and develop their own generalizations from primary source material, from direct observation of social events and processes, and from games and simulations." [17]

In the meantime, government aid increased rapidly during the 1960s. For the first time, Congress approved federal scholarships for needy undergraduates under the Higher Education Act

[17] Gerald Ponder, "The More Things Change . . .: The Status of Social Studies," *Educational Leadership,* April 1979, p. 515. The magazine is published by the Association for Education and Curriculum Development, Alexandria, Va.

of 1965. The Elementary and Secondary Education Act (ESEA), passed the same year, provided financial assistance for education programs such as the preschool "Head Start" project, aimed at increasing the opportunities of disadvantaged children in inner cities and rural areas. Federal funds for education almost doubled in 1957-64 and more than doubled in 1965-1966 as a result of the ESEA; it raised the federal contribution to education from $1.1 billion in 1963-64 to $3 billion in 1967-68, increasing the federal share of public education expenses from 5 percent to 9 percent.

Switch From 'Open Education' to Basics

By the late 1960s the problems that had been highlighted by Sputnik — that of a general decline in academic standards — had receded from the national spotlight, overshadowed by concerns about the quality of education available to the poor, minorities and the handicapped. By 1968 the war in Vietnam had begun to erode available public funds for education, which started to lag behind the growth in student population.[18] Federal support for research and development and science education also continued dropping. These declines, along with demographic changes, ended a period of rapid expansion of college and university science and engineering departments. Federal support for graduate fellowships in science and engineering also went down from 1968 onward. NSF support for teacher training institutes and curriculum development dropped off in the early 1970s and by mid-decade had virtually disappeared.

The decline in federal support for science education coincided with a shift in emphasis in many of the nation's schools, which were greatly influenced by the country's anti-establishment mood in the late 1960s. Ironically, the emphasis on learning through discovery and inquiry that had gained popularity through the NSF's curriculum development efforts had by this time begun to feed into the building of the open education movement. And, according to Diane Ravitch, it had gained enough momentum by 1967 to create an academic laxity similar to the one many educators complained about in the 1950s.

In response to student demand for greater flexibility and "relevance," colleges began lowering their entrance requirements and high schools began abolishing certain course requirements. "As requirements fell," Ravitch wrote in *The New Republic*, "the notion of a common curriculum was undermined. To maintain student interest, courses in traditional subjects were fragmented into electives and mini-courses . . . and

[18] See "Debating National Education Policy: The Question of Standards," American Enterprise Institute for Public Policy Research, 1981.

requirements in the 'hard' subjects like mathematics, science and foreign language were eased or eliminated." [19]

The brightest and most motivated students continued taking advanced college-preparatory courses but others found they could easily avoid the most challenging courses. Ravitch attributes lower teacher expectations of students to uncertainty about what students should study, which undermined the teachers' sense of purpose and authority. This situation, added to the general student unrest and societal permissiveness in the 1960s, made it increasingly difficult for them to impose demands. Truancy and discipline problems increased and homework and essays fell into disfavor.

In the mid-1970s, however, educators snapped to attention when they noticed declines in SAT scores. The back-to-basics movement, with its emphasis on fundamentals and traditional teaching methods, took hold when educators realized that the innovations of the late 1960s and early 1970s were not yielding desired results. An offshoot of the trend back to basics was the adoption by many states of standardized, minimal competency tests. Now 38 states use competency testing, which is a requirement for high school graduation in 17 of them. [20]

In the late 1970s came a new surge of interest in private secondary schools. Parents became disenchanted with public schools because of their apparent failure to educate children both intellectually and morally. That has been a large factor in the recent support by many, including the Reagan administration, of tuition tax credits for private schools. [21] The Republican Party's 1980 platform championed tuition tax credits as "a matter of fairness, especially for low-income families, most of whom would be free for the first time to choose for their children those schools which best correspond to their own cultural and moral values." Opponents of the tuition tax credits argue, however, they will undermine the already beleaguered public school system. Two proposed tax credit programs have failed in Congress since 1978, and recently a third was introduced by Senate Finance Committee Chairman Robert Dole, R-Kan., on behalf of the administration. Although the outlook for any tax credit proposal is doubtful this year, the issue is expected to remain alive throughout this decade.

Evaluation of Sputnik-Inspired Changes

In 1978 the National Science Foundation completed three studies on local, state and national efforts to reform elementary

[19] Diane Ravitch, "The Schools We Deserve," *The New Republic*, April 18, 1981, p. 26.
[20] See "Education's Return to Basics," *E.R.R.*, 1975 Vol. II, pp. 667-684, and "Competency Tests," *E.R.R.*, 1978 Vol. II, pp. 603-620.
[21] See "Tuition Tax Credits," *E.R.R.*, 1981 Vol. II, pp. 595-612, and "Private School Resurgence," *E.R.R.*, 1979 Vol. I, pp. 285-304.

and secondary school curricula since Sputnik to find out what had happened in science, math and social studies education.[22] The conditions they found in 1978 have not significantly changed since then, according to most educators. Apparently math instruction has changed very little since 1955. The new math that grew out of NSF-supported efforts was widely used for a short time but fell quickly into disfavor because it was baffling to most students, teachers and parents, and failed to get results. Over a third of the principals and about a fourth of the supervisors and teachers surveyed by the NSF said the new math had been a waste of time and money.

Twenty-four years ago James Killian, President Eisenhower's first special assistant for science and technology, said: "We must modernize and invigorate science education, strive for a higher degree of scientific literacy among the rank and file of Americans, and correct the erroneous view that science is only vocational, materialistic and anti-humanistic."[23] However, according to NSF's studies, there is little evidence that these goals for science education have ever been translated into any long-lasting curriculum or classroom practice.

In a summary of NSF's findings that appeared in the March 1979 issue of *Educational Leadership,* educators Robert E. Yager and Ronald Stodghill wrote, "The science curriculum exists as the facts and concepts that are traditionally packaged as textbooks.... Little real curriculum planning or school articulation of science materials has occurred." [24] The inquiry and discovery method of teaching math and science that was promoted heavily after Sputnik is apparently not used much, nor are the materials designed to promote those techniques.

The impact of NSF-supported national science programs, which de-emphasized practical applied science and emphasized basic concepts and processes, has been negligible. About a third of the schools surveyed use or have used one of the several NSF-developed elementary programs, and about the same number of high schools have used NSF-funded chemistry and physics courses. But teachers who have tried the NSF curricula seem to be slowly returning to the old courses. Use of these programs had increased until 1970 and then started declining, mostly because the material was too difficult and abstract for most students.

---

[22] See S. L. Helgeson and others, "The Status of Pre-College Science, Mathematics, and Social Studies Educational Practices in U.S. Schools: An Overview and Summaries of Three Studies," U.S. Government Printing Office, 1978.
[23] Quoted by Oto Sturzenegger, *op. cit.,* p. 13.
[24] Robert E. Yager and Ronald Stodghill, "School Science in the Age of Science," *Educational Leadership,* March 1979, pp. 439, 440. Yager is head of the Science Education Center at the University of Iowa; Stodghill is associate superintendent of instructional support services for St. Louis public schools.

Post-Sputnik Education

Philip Jackson, professor of education and behavioral science at the University of Chicago, believes that the climate of the country in the late 1960s was a crucial factor in the decline in use of these Sputnik-inspired programs. Science and technology were seen as dehumanizing forces during this period of Vietnam War protest, denial of traditional values and interest in alternative lifestyles. According to Jackson, the most significant impact of NSF-funded science courses seems to have been that much of their content and methods has been absorbed into commercially published textbooks.

The expensive and ambitious social studies program that emerged after Sputnik called "Man: A Course of Study" is used in less than 5 percent of the schools today, Diane Ravitch told Editorial Research Reports. She explained: "It was basically driven out of the schools because it was so controversial. It used anthropological concepts that a lot of people found extremely hard to understand, and a lot of parents found it objection-

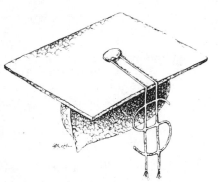

able and subversive." The National Science Foundation has concluded that little has changed in social studies since the 1950s. In high schools, history and geography rather than social science are still the dominant subjects. In elementary schools, social studies serve mostly as an opportunity to teach reading and writing. A Colorado teacher reported, "We do math and reading in the morning when the kids are fresh. We do science and social studies in the afternoon, if there's a chance." [25]

Many educators have concluded that although the NSF-funded curricula may have been excellent in themselves, there was a failure in translating them so they could be used by most teachers. It was the better teachers who attended teacher-training institutes; the ones who needed help most did not participate. However, educators say that rather than a failure in training teachers, the curricula reflected more of a failure in understanding how children learn.

Preliminary results of a 1982 NSF study indicate that although the new curricula are not widely used now, they were more successful than most people realized. [26] An analysis was made of 105 studies in the 1960s and 1970s involving 45,000

[25] Quoted by Gerald Ponder, *op. cit.*, p. 516.
[26] Ronald Anderson and others, "Preliminary Results of Project NSF SED 80-12310," National Science Foundation, 1982.

students. The researchers compared students enrolled in traditional curricula with those enrolled in NSF curricula. On every measure, including achievement, attitude and process skills, the latter group of students scored 14 percent higher overall. According to National Science Teachers Association President Sarah Klein, what is most significant is that students from low socio-economic groups scored 24 percent higher using the new curricula.

Debate Over Responsibilities

F EW WOULD contest the prevailing belief that scientific illiteracy resulting from problems in math and science education hurts the nation's quest for supremacy in high technology. Where the solutions lie, however, is the subject of debate. Educators typically believe that the federal government has a major responsibility in funding science education. But the Reagan administration is reducing the federal financing of education at all levels.

Of the $20.4 million appropriated for the National Science Foundation's 1982 science education activities, $15 million was for graduate fellowships.[27] The National Science Teachers Association points out that since graduate fellowship support is basically support for graduate research, the National Science Foundation has essentially eliminated its science education activities. "The administration has successfully forced NSF to abandon one of its missions," Sarah Klein told a House Appropriations Committee hearing on the 1983 budget.

While the NSTA concedes that the government alone cannot solve the problem of low salaries for science and math teachers, for example, it says the government can help reduce the severity of teacher shortages. It proposes NSF scholarships for math and science teachers, NSF-supported programs of publicity on the need for teachers, NSF-supported courses and workshops for marginally qualified teachers and science consultants, and partial funding of microcomputers in schools.

What the NSF has done is establish a Commission on Precollege Education in Mathematics, Science and Technology, in the words of its charter, to "define a national agenda for improving math and science education in this country." The commission, the charter adds, "will develop an action plan that

[27] Science education funds were cut from $77 million in 1980 to a proposed $15 million for 1983.

will include a definition of appropriate roles and responsibilities of federal, state and local governments, professional and scientific societies, and the private sector in addressing this problem of national dimension."

The National Education Association is also in favor of strong federal support. A bill it drafted, called the American Defense Education Act and introduced in Congress in June, is a modern version of the National Defense Education Act. NEA's bill would have the federal government provide incentives to local school districts to improve instruction in math, science, communication skills, foreign languages and new technologies. A unique feature of the bill is that although its provisions would be administered under the Department of Education, the Department of Defense would project personnel training needs of the armed forces.

"The crisis is upon us," said Denis Doyle of the American Enterprise Institute, "and it is being compounded by the administration's decision to further reduce higher education spending, *without* [his emphasis] proposing a workable alternative. This is precisely the time when increases in human capital investment are most needed. It takes 20 years to train the next generation of engineers, scientists and linguists." [28]

Doyle supports a kind of GI Bill of Rights in reverse, first proposed by Boston University President John Silber. Instead of college aid to individuals for past service — as in the case of military veterans — funds would be made available prospectively. Students who became doctors, nurses and teachers, for example, would have their college-aid debts canceled by working in those professions. Students who received aid but pursued other careers would repay their aid funds through an income tax surcharge. There are existing but limited programs for medical and nursing students.

Potential Roles for States and Industry

While the federal government has stated its concern about science and math education, it is looking to industry, the states and local school districts for their help. Secretary of Education Terrel H. Bell has called on states and local schools to set up task forces to "develop a means of parting with the single salary schedule to help stem the erosion, in fact, the bleeding off, of mathematics and science teachers into other disciplines." [29] The alternative to a single salary schedule — that is, all teachers being paid equally — would be payment by specialty, whereby a

---

[28] Writing in *The Washington Post*, March 10, 1982.
[29] Address to National Convocation on Preschool Education in Mathematics and Science.

math teacher, for example, could earn more than an art teacher. Although some schools are considering differential salary scales, the American Federation of Teachers opposes such a move, claiming that pay differences would be too small to keep significant numbers of math and science teachers in schools but large enough to cause friction with other teachers.[30]

To encourage industry to help out, several members of Congress have introduced bills focusing on teacher and equipment shortages. Rep. Fortney H. "Pete" Stark, D-Calif., would increase tax deductions available to companies that donate computers to elementary and secondary schools. Currently, full deductions for such scientific equipment are allowed only if it is given to colleges and universities. If Stark's bill passes, the chairman and co-founder of Apple Computer Inc., Steven A. Jobbs, said he would donate a new computer to every school in the country. A bill introduced by Sen. Lloyd Bentsen, D-Texas, offers tax deductions to companies that donate equipment to vocational schools.

Even without generous tax advantages some companies have already begun to help schools out, acknowledging that industry is partially responsible for the current teacher shortage, having lured away many present and future instructors with generous pay offers. The Exxon Foundation, for example, has donated $15 million to help engineering schools obtain and keep faculty members, and Motorola gave $1.2 million to Arizona State University's engineering program.

Sen. John Glenn, D-Ohio, and Rep. Dave McCurdy, D-Okla., each introduced two bills supported by the National Association of Secondary School Principals. One would give tax credits to firms that hire public school science and math teachers during the summer — to augment their paychecks so they could remain in teaching — or let their employees who are former teachers return to the classroom to teach 10 hours a week. The other bill would provide 7 percent loans to science and math teachers. A quarter of the debt would be written off for each year the loan recipient teaches.

The idea of enticing students to teach math and science by awarding them forgivable loans is catching on in the states as well. College students in Kentucky this fall will be eligible for $2,500-a-year loans they will not have to repay if they teach science or math in elementary or secondary schools. A new program in Alabama will award loans covering tuition, room, board and books. Students will not have to repay these loans if

---

[30] AFT proposes that all salaries be raised uniformly and that schools test teachers in glutted subject areas, such as history and the arts, for math or science aptitude. If the teachers are willing and able, they could be retrained rather than laid off.

they become high-school teachers of math, chemistry, physics, biology or general science.

Schools Raising Academic Requirements

Aside from adopting minimum competency tests for high school students, increasing numbers of states have begun raising their standards for incoming teachers. Recent changes in teacher licensing requirements have been adopted in Texas, Delaware, New Mexico, New Jersey, Maryland and Connecticut. Stiffer curriculum requirements also seem to be making a comeback. Texas recently eliminated extraneous courses from its requirements. California is proposing that every student have three years of math and two of science in order to graduate. In Florida a similar proposal would require four years of math and four of science.

While some experts are rethinking graduation requirements, particularly in math and science, others are considering more basic changes in the structure of the American school system. In 1959 James B. Conant's influential book *The American High School Today* attacked the quality of education for academically gifted students and spurred the creation of large centralized high schools offering both academic and vocational instruction.[31] A new study of secondary education by the Carnegie Foundation for the Advancement of Teaching, which will be released next year, will conclude that students would be better served by smaller specialized schools that could address their needs more directly.

Whatever the answers are to improving children's education, transformations will not occur overnight. Money, and who should provide how much, is only part of the problem. Diane Ravitch wrote, "The problem is that we lack consensus about whether there should be a common curriculum, whether there are knowledge and skills that everyone should have. If we believed that it was important to have a highly literate public, to have a public capable of understanding history and politics and economics, to have citizens who are knowledgeable about science and technology, to have a society in which the powers of verbal communication are developed systematically and intentionally, then we would know what we wanted of our schools. Until we do, we get the schools we deserve, which accurately reflect our own confusion about the value of education." [32] Growing alarm about scientific and technological illiteracy, which experts see as seriously endangering our national prospects, could — as Sputnik did in 1957 — clarify this confusion and serve as a catalyst for an educational overhaul.

---

[31] James B. Conant, *The American High School Today* (1967).
[32] Diane Ravitch, *op. cit.*, p. 27.

Selected Bibliography

Books

Ailes, Catherine P. and Francis W. Rushing, *The Science Race: Training and Utilization of Scientists and Engineers, US and USSR,* Crane Russak, 1982.

Armbruster, Frank, *Our Children's Crippled Future: How American Education Has Failed,* New York Times Book Co., 1977.

Conant, James B., *The American High School Today,* McGraw-Hill, 1967.

Articles

Cohen, David K. and Barbara Neufeld, "The Failure of High Schools and the Progress of Education," *Daedalus,* summer 1981.

Educational Leadership, selected issues.

Henderson, Richard P., "High Tech: Help Wanted," *Enterprise* (journal of the National Association of Manufacturers), March 1982.

Ravitch, Diane, "The Schools We Deserve," *The New Republic,* April 18, 1981.

Sturzenegger, Otto, "We'd Better Do Something About Science Education," *Industry Week,* July 26, 1982.

Wellborn, Stanley N., "Johnny Can't Count — The Dangers for the U.S.," *U.S. News & World Report,* Feb. 15, 1982.

Reports and Studies

Bush, Vannevar, "Science — The Endless Frontier, 1950-1960," National Science Foundation, 1945 (reprinted 1980).

"Education in the Sciences: A Developing Crisis," American Association for the Advancement of Science," 1982.

Editorial Research Reports: "America's Employment Outlook," 1982 Vol. I, p. 387; "Educating Gifted Children," 1979 Vol. II, p. 119; "Education's Return to Basics," 1975 Vol. II, p. 661.

"Intergovernmentalizing the Classroom: Federal Involvement in Elementary and Secondary Education," Advisory Commission on Intergovernmental Relations, 1981.

"Science and Engineering Education for the 1980s and Beyond," National Science Foundation and the Department of Education, 1980.

"The Status of Pre-College Science, Mathematics, and Social Studies Educational Practices in U.S. Schools: An Overview and Summaries of Three Studies," National Science Foundation, U.S. Government Printing Office, 1978.

Cover drawing by Staff Artist Robert Redding;
p. 75 graph by Staff Artist Cheryl Rowe;
p. 79 drawing by George Rebh.

ILLITERACY IN AMERICA

by

Roger Thompson

June 24
1 9 8 3

ILLITERACY IN AMERICA

EACH YEAR 850,000 students drop out of school. Most of them cannot read well enough to follow TV dinner instructions; they are too weak in math to compute sales tax. Thousands more who do manage to graduate are no better off; their diplomas mock the system. Together they swell the ranks of an almost invisible underclass of functional illiterates — as many as 23 million Americans, according to one estimate *(see below)*. "Not only are most people unaware of the [illiteracy] problem, but those who are illiterate understandably try to hide it," observed Rep. Paul Simon, D-Ill., who conducted congressional hearings on illiteracy last fall.

Prospects for reducing the number of students who fall through the educational cracks are not immediately promising. The National Commission on Excellence in Education recently concluded that the education of all children is so deplorable that the "nation is at risk." "The educational foundations of our society are ... being eroded by a rising tide of mediocrity," the commission reported *(see box, p. 88)*. One indication of this erosion is the incidence of illiteracy among 17-year-olds, estimated at 13 percent.

The problem appears even worse among adults. Another study determined that one of every five American adults, some 23 million, flunk "the simplest tests of reading, writing and comprehension." They cannot respond to a help-wanted ad, read directions on a medicine bottle, write a check or make change. That was the conclusion of the Adult Performance Level study, released in 1975 by researchers at the University of Texas at Austin. The study, based on a nationwide survey of 7,500 individuals, remains the most frequently cited report on illiteracy.[1] According to Secretary of Education Terrel H. Bell, there is no reason to believe the number of illiterates has diminished.

Army personnel specialist Nora Kinzer told Simon's subcommittee that 17,500 recruit applicants flunked a fifth-grade-level reading test in 1981. Although the volunteer Army has stopped taking recruits with less than fifth-grade reading

---

[1] "Adult Functional Competency: A Summary," Division of Extension, University of Texas at Austin, 1975. The figure of 850,000 student drop-outs is a Department of Education estimate.

ability, the number of soldiers taking remedial courses increased from 166,000 in 1979 to 220,000 in 1981. The costs of remedial instruction then reached $70 million. Without remedial work, Kinzer said, those soldiers cannot even begin the training they need to handle sophisticated military equipment.[2]

Nation's Cost: Billions of Dollars Yearly

Literacy also has become a concern of American corporations. The New York-based Center for Public Resources (CPR) said that in a survey it conducted last year, three-quarters of 184 responding corporations reported that employee errors in reading, writing and math had forced them to establish basic skills programs. An "informed guess" at the price tag for such efforts nationwide is more than $10 billion, said Susan Raymond, a CPR vice president who is the author of the study.[3]

Basic skills competency has become a corporate priority only recently, she said, explaining: "High school grads are going into a work place that is much more communications-oriented, much more information-oriented, much more group-working-oriented. And it requires more speaking, listening, mathematics and reasoning skills."[4] Knowledge of specific skills is not as im-

---

[2] Testifying Sept. 21, 1982, before the House Subcommittee on Postsecondary Education.
[3] Center for Public Resources, "Basic Skills in the U.S. Work Force," 1982, pp. 25-27. The center designs and implements cooperative projects between public and private concerns.
[4] For background, see "The Big Business of Employee Education," *E.R.R.*, 1981 Vol. 1, pp. 3-15.

portant as the ability to think and solve problems, Raymond continued.

Illiteracy exacts a high price in other ways. The authors of a book on adult illiteracy, published in 1979,[5] put the annual cost of welfare programs and unemployment compensation due to illiteracy at $6 billion. They pointed to welfare statistics showing that persons with less than a high school education are far more likely than others to be out of work and applying for public assistance. The prison population also reflects the social cost for illiteracy. According to the author's findings, about 75 percent of the inmates had not completed high school, as opposed to 38 percent of the total adult population. More than one-third have not finished the eighth grade. The nation spends $6.6 billion a year to keep 750,000 illiterates in jail, said Barbara Bush, wife of Vice President George Bush and a crusader against illiteracy. "I'm trying to remind people that there's a correlation between crime and illiteracy, between illiteracy and unemployment." [6]

Racial, Ethnic, Geographic Concentrations

Who are the nation's illiterates? The Adult Performance Level study found they are likely to be among the 45 million adults who — according to Census Bureau calculations — do not have a high school diploma. Typically they are poor and members of racial or ethnic minority groups. Illiteracy is most pervasive in nine Southern or border states — Alabama, Arkansas, Georgia, Kentucky, Mississippi, North Carolina, South Carolina, Tennessee and West Virginia — where over half of the adults have not completed high school.[7]

The APL study found illiteracy equally divided between males and females, but it found significant differences among racial or ethnic groups. Sixteen percent of all whites were estimated to be functionally illiterate, compared to 44 percent of all blacks and 56 percent of all Hispanics. Over the past decade the percentage of school dropouts among white and Hispanic students has increased, while it fell for blacks, as shown in the following Census Bureau findings:

	1970*	1980
White	14.1%	14.9%
Hispanic	30.7	38.8
Black	31.2	21.3

* 1972 for Hispanics

---

[5] Carman St. John Hunter and Dvaid Harman, *Adult Illiteracy in the United States* (1979), p. 51.

[6] Quoted in *The New York Times*, Sept. 16, 1982. Mrs. Bush serves on the board of Laubach Literary Action *(see p. 98)*.

[7] Figures cited by Hunter and Harman, *op. cit.*, pp. 23-56.

Adding to the stream of illiterates dropping out of the schools, the Department of Education estimates that 400,000 legal immigrants, 150,000 refugees and an estimated 800,000 illegal immigrants enter the country each year. Most come from Latin America and Asia. A large percentage are not proficient in either their native language or English.

Concern Over Nation's High-Tech Future

Literacy is not a static concept. On the American frontier, a person who could write his own name was considered literate. Industrial America demanded basic reading and math for survival. The emerging computer-age work place demands "higher order" skills — critical thinking and problem solving. These are tomorrow's basic skills, based on market predictions that by 1990 more than half of the labor force will be employed in technical and white-collar jobs. The schools, however, are losing ground in the struggle to keep education abreast of the times, according to a National Assessment of Educational Progress report.[8] It found the following among the 17-year-olds:

> Average correct responses on inferential comprehension items fell from 64 percent to 62 percent between 1971 and 1980. Inferential comprehension requires readers to draw inferences or make judgments based on ideas not explicitly stated.
>
> Average performance on math problems requiring several steps declined from 33 percent to 29 percent.
>
> Correct responses to science questions dropped from 51 percent to 46 percent. "Clearly we are not cultivating the raw materials, our future workers, who will be vital both for economic progress and ultimately for economic survival," the study concluded.

For large numbers of people thrown out of work by the recession, the future is now. Industry analysts predict that thousands of jobs in steel, rubber, automotive and other heavy industries are gone for good. Retraining offers at least a glimmer of hope for those whose jobs have disappeared. But the Department of Labor estimates that 75 percent of the unemployed lack the basic skills necessary to be retrained for high-technology jobs. The problem of job retraining is particularly vexing in the industrial Midwest, said Professor Louis Ferman, who directs the University of Michigan's Institute for Labor and Industrial Relations.

Mass-production jobs are partly responsible for the retraining difficulty. Assembly-line workers are not expected "to do any-

---

[8] The National Assessment of Educational Progress, funded by the National Institute for Education and administered by the Denver-based Education Commission of the States, periodically surveys the educational achievement of America's 9-, 13- and 17-year-olds in various learning areas.

Varsity Illiteracy

Kevin Ross, a basketball star who attended Creighton University in Omaha for four years, made headlines last September when he enrolled in elementary school. He could barely read and write. "I just don't know how I made it through all those years of school without those skills," said Ross, who left Creighton on academic probation after a knee injury knocked him out of the team lineup. "I sure know how to play basketball, though." *

Ross' story emerged only months before the National Collegiate Athletic Association (NCAA) adopted the tougher eligibility rules for freshman athletes in response to criticism that colleges and universities neglect the academic performance of student athletes.

The NCAA decided Jan. 11 to rule any freshman ineligible for varsity sports if he or she had not scored 700 out of a possible 1,600 points on the Scholastic Aptitude Test, or 15 out of a possible 36 points on the American College Testing Program's exam. However, if the student was making satisfactory progress toward a degree, he or she could become eligible the following year. A second new rule stipulates that an athlete must have achieved a high school grade point average of 2.0 on a 4.0-scale. Both rules take effect in the fall of 1986.

The rules touched off a storm of controversy, particularly from the heads of predominantly black colleges who contend that standardized tests such as the SAT are inappropriate as standards for college admission or athletic eligibility. These officials note that the vast majority of students in their institutions, athletes or not, would not meet the standard of a combined score of 700.

"Thirty-six percent of the students in our colleges are getting 350 on the verbal [section of the SAT], and 45 percent are getting that on the math," said Alan Kirschner, director of research and government affairs for the United Negro College Fund, an organization of 42 traditionally black colleges.**

* Quoted in the *Chicago Tribune*, Jan. 11, 1983.
** Quoted in *The New York Times*, Jan. 14, 1983.

---

thing that requires conceptual skills," Ferman said in an interview. As a result, reading and writing skills atrophy. While unemployment in December hit a post-Depression high of 10.7 percent, jobs in computer, business machine and data processing firms have gone begging. This situation has set off cries of alarm from the scientific community that the schools are graduating "a new generation of Americans that is scientifically and technologically illiterate." [9]

The National Science Foundation and the American Association for the Advancement of Science, saying the quality of science instruction has deteriorated, have warned that the

[9] National Commission on Excellence in Education, p. 10.

United States might be without the trained people it needs to compete in the world economy.[10] Many experienced math and science teachers are abandoning the classroom for better-paying jobs in industry. Math teachers are in short supply in nearly every state. A 1982 survey by the National Council of Supervisors of Mathematics found that 22 percent of all high school teaching posts in math were vacant nationwide and 26 percent were filled by teachers uncertified in mathematics.

President Reagan has joined the chorus of persons seeking to upgrade math and science instruction. "The education of American schoolchildren in science and math has reached such a deplorable state that it threatens the nation's military and economic security," he said in the State of the Union address to Congress on Jan. 25. Saying that America is lagging behind Japan in educating engineers, he called for "a quality education initiative to encourage a substantial upgrading of math and science instruction. . . ."

Search for Causes, Remedies

OBTAINING an accurate count of the functional illiterates in America is not yet possible mainly because there is more than one definition of illiteracy. The Census Bureau considers anyone who completed the fifth grade among the literate. By this measurement, only about a million persons, one-half of one percent of the population, are illiterate. But the consensus among researchers is that literacy cannot be measured simply by counting grades of school completed. The best approach, they contend, is to measure literacy by the ability to handle everyday reading and math. This is the method used by the Adult Performance Level study.

The U.S. Office (now Department) of Education commissioned the APL study in 1971 at a time when Congress was preparing to mount an ambitious national program to eliminate adult illiteracy within a decade. The findings astonished even those who were familiar with the illiteracy problem: Twenty percent of the persons interviewed could not understand a notice describing a store's check-cashing policy. Fourteen percent were unable to fill out a check correctly. Thirteen percent did not address an envelope well enough to ensure it would reach the desired destination. Twenty-one percent could not follow instructions which read, "Take two pills twice a day." An equal number could not determine how often to have a home

[10] For background, see "Post-Sputnik Education," *E.R.R.*, 1982 Vol. II, pp. 653-672.

inspected for termites when a government brochure advised, "periodic inspections should be made at least every six months if you live where termites are common."

The study concluded that traditional grade-level measures of literacy were flawed beyond usefulness. It recommended instead that educators use the concept of functional literacy — the ability to perform carefully defined tasks — as the basis for curriculum development and student testing. It proved to be a timely recommendation.

Demand for Basics and Competency Tests

By the mid-1970s, parents were demanding stricter educational standards to counter declining student achievement. Scholastic Aptitude Test scores for college-bound students had been on a yearly skid for more than a decade. Even non-readers could get high school diplomas, prompting a flurry of educational malpractice suits from outraged parents. "Back to basics" became the rallying cry of an aroused public that went over the heads of local school boards and appealed directly to state legislatures for action. Thirty-six states responded by

"Pardon me, but where is the Functional Illiterates Counseling Center?"

enacting laws requiring students to pass minimum competency tests to receive a high school diploma. No other educational movement has been so pervasive and effective so quickly.[11]

Competency testing was modeled on the performance-based approach to literacy used by the Adult Performance Level study. Students are required to read road maps, add grocery bills, explain simple tax forms, plan trips based on mass transit schedules, and the like. In North Carolina, the second state (after Florida) to make competency testing a high school graduation requirement, the results have been encouraging. Ninety percent of the 11th graders who took the first competency test in the fall of 1978 passed the reading section. By last fall, the first-time success rate had climbed to 92.8 percent, said William Brown, a special assistant for research in the state Department of Education.

---

[11] See "Education Returns to the Basics," *E.R.R.*, 1975 Vol. II, pp. 665-684, and "Competency Tests," *E.R.R.*, 1978 Vol. II, pp. 601-620.

The public outcry for tougher standards also affected teachers. Parents complained that school systems hired and retained teachers who themselves lacked proficiency in basic skills. As a result, 19 states[12] now require teachers to pass minimum competency tests, based largely on traditional academic criteria, to earn certification. The tests are intended to screen out incompetent would-be teachers and identify weak teacher-training programs. The pass rate for Louisiana's future teachers has risen from 53 to 75 percent since testing began in 1978. In Florida, 84 percent of the college students who took the test last October passed.[13]

In each state, minority students are failing in disproportionate numbers. While the overall pass rate in Florida was 84 percent, 90 percent of the whites passed but only 51 percent of the Hispanics and 35 percent of the blacks. Critics charge the tests are culturally and racially biased. And there is growing concern that widespread use of the tests could drive black and Hispanic teachers out of the schools. "Our contention is that minorities have not been taught those particular skills," said Walter Mercer, a professor of education at predominantly black Florida A&M University. Ralph Turlington, the state school superintendent, replied: "We're not going to bring about student learning if we have teachers who are not readers, who can't handle writing and can't handle math." [14]

Attack on 'Look-Say' Reading Instruction

Many educators caution that the decline in student achievement is far too complex a matter for a set of tests to remedy. A blue-ribbon panel that studied the decline in Scholastic Aptitude Test (SAT) scores concluded in 1977 that multiple factors must be taken into consideration. These include the break-up of the traditional American family, national trauma caused by the turbulent Vietnam War years, the impact of television and teen-age drug use and declining academic standards.

At least one critic of public education refuses to equivocate. The "look-and-say" method of reading instruction at the elementary grades is at fault, argues Rudolf Flesch, who has preached the same educational sermon since 1955, the year his book *Why Johnny Can't Read* appeared. In *Why Johnny Still Can't Read* (1981), he argues anew that that look-and-say is a "fradulent, pernicious gimmick." "Twenty-five years ago I stud-

---

[12] Alabama, Arizona, Arkansas, California, Connecticut, Colorado, Florida, Georgia, Louisiana, Mississippi, New Mexico, New York, North Carolina, Oklahoma, South Carolina, Tennessee, Texas, Virginia and West Virginia.
[13] Figures cited in *U.S. News & World Report*, "What's Wrong With Our Teachers?" March 14, 1983, p. 40.
[14] Remarks made in interviews on "The MacNeil-Lehrer Report," PBS-TV, May 9, 1983, p. 2.

Merit Pay Debate

Merit pay for teachers began taking shape as a 1984 presidential campaign issue soon after the National Commission on Excellence in Education recommended it as a necessary step to make teaching more professionally attractive.

President Reagan subsequently has expressed strong support for performance-based pay raises on several occasions, provided that the states and school districts pay the tab. The National Education Association, American Federation of Teachers and other teacher organizations oppose it, arguing that it will not work fairly. And Democratic presidential hopefuls, whose party traditionally gets teacher support, are left with politically tough choices to make.

Reagan has embraced as a possible national model the merit pay plan pushed by Republican Gov. Lamar Alexander of Tennessee. The plan would classify teachers as apprentice, professional, senior or master. Forty percent would make the top two grades and receive raises between $2,000 and $7,000. The average Tennessee teacher with 20 years of experience now earns about $17,000 a year.

The governor said the program would cost $110 million a year by the time it was fully implemented. "If you want the best results, you hire the best people. In this day and time, you can't hire the best people with a pay scale that rewards mediocrity," Alexander said. His enthusiasm for the idea, however, did not rub off on the Tennessee General Assembly. Lawmakers shelved the plan in May for additional study until they reconvene next February. Alexander attributed the defeat to the teachers' unions.

Willard McGuire, president of the National Education Association, contends that merit pay will not work because no one has come up with a fair way to assess teacher performance. "All teachers are woefully underpaid, so you can't even talk about adding salary incentives until you have adequate pay for everyone," McGuire said.*

* Alexander and McGuire were quoted in *U.S. News & World Report,* June 20, 1983, pp. 61-62.

ied American methods of teaching reading and warned against educational catastrophe. Now it has happened," he writes.

Flesch contends that a "phonics-first" method is the only sure way to make children independent readers. With phonics, children are first taught the mechanics of reading vowels, consonants and combinations of the two. These become building blocks for learning to read. With the look-and-say method, children learn to recognize certain words by sight before they are taught the mechanics. In his later book, Flesch said 85 percent of all schools were still using the look-and-say method despite overwhelming evidence favoring phonics-first. He said he had found 124 comparative studies conducted since 1911, and not one showed that look-and-say was superior.

In their defense, educators argue that phonics is not a method of teaching, but an aid to be blended into a total reading program that also includes look-and-say. Children learn in many different ways, and it is important not to assume one way works best for all, they argue. Besides, textbook publishers point out, since the debate over phonics erupted 28 years ago, phonics no longer is left out of reading instruction.

Whatever the merits of the two approaches, one thing is clear. The books that students read are not as demanding as they once were. For a decade, textbook publishers have been writing their materials with shorter sentences and words, more pictures, larger print and wider margins. Many texts now are written on a level two grades below the one for which they are intended. In the trade, this is known as "dumbing down." [15] Once out of school, students accustomed to "dumbed down" materials may find even the daily paper too challenging. Reading experts and publishers who assembled for an American Enterprise Institute seminar in Washington last fall expressed concern that a large number of young people choose to be "a-literate." They know how to read but don't.

Fluctuating Commitment to Adult Education

The federal government has had an on-again, off-again commitment to literacy training since World War I when the armed forces set up literacy programs for thousands of draftees. During the Depression, Washington funded literacy classes through the Works Progress Administration. Literacy again became a national issue as the country prepared for World War II. The armed services rejected 100,000 of the first two million men called up because they were illiterate. Eventually, 303,000 men received Army literacy training and 254,000 of those passed fourth-grade reading tests.[16]

In each instance, direct government involvement in literacy training ended when the period of national crisis passed. The prevailing feeling was that illiteracy was a matter of an individual's bad luck. The federal attitude changed in 1964 at the dawning of Lyndon B. Johnson's "Great Society." Concern for the underprivileged led Congress to initiate Adult Basic Education programs. Funding over the years increased from an initial $5 million to a high of $100 million in 1980. The Reagan administration proposed funding of $85 million in the current fiscal year, but Congress raised the figure to $96 million.

[15] Paul Copperman, *The Literacy Hoax* (1978), p. 79.
[16] Figures cited by Edwin H. Smith, in *Literacy Education for Adolescents and Adults* (1970), p. 5.

Enrollment grew from 38,000 in 1965 to 2.2 million in 1982. Of those, 1.6 million were in classes learning skills no higher than the ninth-grade level, according to the Department of Education. The benefits have been impressive. In 1980, approximately 90,000 participants reported they got jobs as a result of being in the program, and about 55,000 others were promoted to better jobs. In addition, 115,000 adults enrolled in other training programs at the conclusion of their adult education studies, almost 35,000 were removed from public assistance rolls, 30,000 obtained drivers' licenses and 25,000 registered to vote for the first time.

At best, adult education reaches only a fraction of those who need it. A more ambitious program once was tried without success. The national Right to Read program, launched by the Nixon administration in 1971, set out to eliminate illiteracy within a decade. It was intended to serve as a catalyst to stimulate state and private sector efforts. The program, however, was a miserable failure, said its former director, Gilbert B. Schiffman, now a professor of education at Johns Hopkins University in Baltimore.

"The illiteracy problem is very severe. It's a national disgrace," Schiffman said in an interview. "Right to Read was going to solve the problem by 1980. It was to be the equivalent of our commitment to go to the moon. But I think the maximum we ever got was $30 million. We had large ideas, but a small budget and no political clout."

While the federal government channeled only a trickle of money into Right to Read, it was pouring billions into compensatory education programs in public elementary schools. The money flowed through Title I of the Elementary and Secondary Education Act, which Congress passed in 1965 specifically to improve teaching of basic skills to children from low-income homes. Between 1965 and 1981, the program pumped $29.6 billion into the schools.[17] That investment appears to have paid dividends. The National Assessment of Educational Progress has found that while all nine-year-olds made significant gains in

[17] Figures cited by Gene I. Maeroff in *Dont' Blame the Kids* (1982), p. 8.

reading over the last decade, black nine-year-olds made by far the largest gains. Despite the gains, blacks remain below the national average.[18]

Working quietly behind the scenes all the while have been volunteer adult literacy organizations. The two major ones are Laubach Literacy Action and Literacy Volunteers of America. Both are based in Syracuse, N.Y. Literacy Volunteers claims 17,000 students in 165 programs in 26 states. Laubach's tutors reach about 50,000 students a year through 600 projects in 48 states. For all their work, the organizations feel more frustration than reward.

"We are not making any impact on the problem right now," Peter A. Waite, Laubach's executive director, said in an interview. "If the American public were knowledgeable of the situation, they'd be aghast."

Remedial Efforts Under Way

DESPITE efforts currently being made by volunteer organizations, schools, business and government, the consensus is that illiteracy is not yielding to the programs designed to attack it. One major problem is that high technology is raising the "functional literacy" threshold. "It's hard to hit a moving target," remarks Paul Delker, the Department of Education's director of adult education. Another obstacle is that there simply is no quick fix for illiteracy, no single program that will wipe it out in a relatively short period of time.

Adults who missed the basics develop layers of bad habits to mask their inability to read and handle simple math. They avoid looking at billboards, street signs, store window advertisements and other sources of written information most people take for granted. Those who have some reading ability learn to guess when they come upon unfamiliar words. Consequently, years of bad habits must be overcome before adults begin to show real progress at reading. Even then, the progress is slow. Most experts agree that about 100 hours of study will take an adult student up one grade level in general reading ability, about the same as the average child requires.

Public schools continue to look for the right teaching techniques to ensure that every student masters the basics at an early age. One of the most promising approaches has been adopted by the Chicago public schools. Last year the city

---

[18] National Assessment of Educational Progress, "Reading, Science and Mathematics Trends, A Closer Look," December 1982.

schools implemented a "mastery learning program" based on the idea that all children can learn to read and do math, but that it takes some longer than others.

The system was developed in the 1960s by a University of Chicago professor of education, Benjamin Bloom. It requires students to pass tests on each concept before they advance to the next learning assignment. Those who fail are taught and tested again. So far, officials are pleased with the results. Standardized tests show the average 11- and 12-year-old student last year made a full year's progress in reading and math. Similar results elsewhere in the nation over the years have persuaded hundreds of schools systems to adopt the mastery learning approach.[19]

Renewed emphasis on the basics, particularly reading, has produced significant increases in achievement test scores in Atlanta, Boston, Houston, Minneapolis, New Orleans, Newark and Philadelphia.[20] Drilling students in the basics of reading and math, however, may have contributed to the decline in their reasoning and analytic skills, the National Assessment of Education Progress reported. Educators already are placing a new emphasis on making critical thinking a part of the curriculum. The University/Urban Schools National Task Force and the College Board have begun a thinking skills program in public schools of New York, Chicago, San Francisco, Detroit, Minneapolis and Memphis. The College Board is putting up $300,000 for the project. The aim is to produce a program that can be used elsewhere.

Drawbacks in Teachers' Pay and Quality

Even as schools attempt to upgrade the quality of instruction, the quality of prospective teachers is dropping. The 1982 Scholastic Aptitude Test (SAT) scores of college-bound seniors heading for education degrees were 81 points below the national average in math and verbal skills, a combined score of 813 out of a possible 1,600 points. Teacher training attracted students who ranked 26th in 29 academic fields surveyed.

Only 5 percent of last year's graduating seniors said they were interested in teaching careers, down from 10 percent just a decade ago, according to a recent study entitled "The American Teacher." The report warns: "Never before in U.S. history has the caliber of those entering the teaching profession been as low as it is today." [21] The study found women, who traditionally

---

[19] Reported in *The New York Times*, "Education Winter Survey," Jan. 9, 1983, p. 23.
[20] Reported in the *Phi Delta Kappan*, December 1982, p. 234. Phi Delta Kappa is a professional fraternity of educators. The College Board administers SATs to college-bound high school students; the task force is a consortium of big city schools and universities.
[21] "The American Teacher," Feistritzer Publications, 1983, p. 59. Dr. Emily Feistritzer is editor and publisher of the Washington-based publications, which include two newsletters on education topics.

Starting Salaries: A Comparison

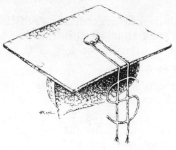

Subject	1980-81	1981-82	Percent Increase
Minimum mean salary for teachers with a bachelor's degree	$11,758	$12,769	4.1
College graduates with a bachelor's degree			
Engineering	20,136	22,368	11.1
Accounting	15,720	16,980	8.0
Sales - Marketing	15,936	17,220	8.1
Business administration	14,100	16,200	14.9
Liberal arts	13,296	15,444	16.2
Chemistry	17,124	19,536	14.1
Mathematics - Statistics	17,604	18,600	5.7
Economics - Finance	14,472	16,884	16.7
Computer sciences	17,712	20,364	15.0
Other fields	17,544	20,028	14.2

Source: "The American Teacher," study by Feistritzer Publications, 1983

provided most of the nation's public school teachers, now have more career choices. Many of "the best and the brightest," the report said, are entering law, medicine, science and business. Only 2.5 percent of the law degrees awarded in 1960 went to women, but 30 percent did in 1980. The women's share of medical degrees rose from 5.5 percent to 23.4 percent in that time.

A survey by the National Education Association in 1981 found that one of every four teachers probably would not again choose teaching as a career. Twenty years earlier, the figure was 8 percent.[22] A 1981 Gallup Poll indicated that two-thirds of America's adults think teaching is not an attractive career for young people.

"What we had before was almost a slave market," said Robert McClure, programs manager for teacher education with the

---

[22] The survey, conducted periodically by the NEA, is entitled "Status of the American Public School Teacher."

Percentage of Women Awarded Degrees

	1950	1960	1970	1980
Medical	1.0	5.5	8.4	23.4
Dentistry	0.7	0.8	0.9	13.3
Law	(NA)	2.5	5.4	30.2
Engineering	0.3	0.4	0.8	8.8
Education	46	64	67	71

Source: *Statistical Abstract of the United States 1981*

National Education Association. "What we must do is make careers in education attractive," he added in an interview. First on almost everyone's list of unattractive features is low pay. The average starting salary for public secondary school teachers in 1981-82 was $12,769, according to the NEA, far below beginner's pay in several other fields *(see table, p. 100)*. Starting salaries not only are low, but salaries for all teachers have not kept pace with inflation. In the decade following the 1971-72 school year, the average teacher's salary rose 81.4 percent while the Consumer Price Index rose 129 percent. Salary increases would help, "The American Teacher" concludes. "But they cannot reverse more than a quarter of a century of steady decline. The teaching profession needs new voices, new directions and new challenges. . . . Unless change is made . . . the [downward] slide will accelerate within the next few years."

Business Training of Its Own Employees

Some businesses already have stepped in to fill the gaps in their employees' educations. The Polaroid Corp. is one of the companies that has started a basic reading and math program, said Polaroid spokeswoman Lynn Stoker. "The worker who doesn't read, who passes preliminary interviews and graduated from high school, he costs us money," she added.[23] The expense of such programs is too much for many businesses to handle. But the Center for Public Resources (CPR) study showed corporate leaders are enthusiastic about a less expensive alternative — working directly with the schools to improve basic skills instruction. School officials surveyed said they are anxious for a corporate helping hand.

As a follow-up on its study, CPR this year will act as a clearinghouse for information on business-school partnerships for improving the basic skills. The center already has a number of examples in its files. One is that of the Security Pacific National Bank of Los Angeles. In conjunction with the California Regional Occupational Program, the bank has developed a

[23] Quoted in *The Washington Post*, Dec. 3, 1982. For background, see "Big Business of Employee Education," *E.R.R.*, 1981 Vol. I, pp. 1-16.

Average Public School Teachers' Salaries

School year	Elementary	Secondary	Total
1972-73	$ 9,893	$10,057	$10,176
1973-74	10,507	11,077	10,778
1974-75	11,334	12,000	11,690
1975-76	12,282	12,947	12,591
1976-77	12,988	13,776	13,352
1977-78	13,860	14,611	14,207
1978-79	14,664	15,441	15,022
1979-80	15,556	16,434	15,951
1980-81	17,204	18,071	17,597
1981-82	18,679	19,712	19,142
1982-83	20,042	21,100	20,531

Source: National Education Association

program to provide entry-level training in 16 skill areas to 2,000 high school students in 70 school districts.

It is this kind of local cooperative effort that is advocated by volunteer literacy organizations such as Laubach Literacy Action. "Building local, private, non-profit partnerships is going to be the key to really reducing functional illiteracy," said Peter A. Waite, Laubach's executive director. "Large amounts of federal dollars won't solve the problem either, although we are looking for more federal support than we have right now."

Waite also rejects the approach favored by Jonathan Kozol in his 1980 book, *Prisoners of Silence.* Kozol calls for a volunteer literacy army of five million college and high school students in an all-out campaign to make 20 million adults functionally literate in less than a year. Similar efforts have been successful in Cuba, Kozol contends. But Waite says "Jonathan Kozol's approach to illiteracy is terribly, terribly naive." Waite argues that it is unrealistic to expect five million students to come forward with sufficient commitment to make such a grandiose project work.

Administration Emphasis on Volunteerism

Volunteerism also appears to be the approach the Reagan administration plans to emphasize. Secretary of Education Bell told the House Subcommittee on Postsecondary Education last fall the country is experiencing a resurgence of the volunteer spirit that should be harnessed to work on the illiteracy problem. "Much of this [volunteer spirit] is due to the personal advocacy role of President Reagan. The return to private sector problem-solving and the demand on local communities to meet human needs has brought a new era of volunteer involvement," Bell said.

Bell also outlined a plan to consolidate the current Adult Basic Education program with vocational education to increase flexibility and decrease costs. According to National Education Association figures, vocational and adult education spending has been cut by $344 million since Reagan took office.

"Not since Sputnik's triumphant flight rattled Americans' faith in our public schools has there been such a clamorous national debate on education."

Time magazine, June 20, 1983

While the Reagan administration does not favor new programs to address adult illiteracy, it supports a renewed effort to boost scientific literacy. The president's fiscal 1984 budget proposed a $75-million crash program to recruit thousands of new math and science teachers for the public schools. The House on March 2 raised that amount to $425 million, of which $250 million would go to public schools, $75 million to colleges for teacher training scholarships and workshops, and $100 million for training engineers and scientists. The Senate Labor and Human Resources Committee on May 11 pushed the price tag even higher, approving nearly $1 billion for math and science and "critical" foreign language education over a two-year period.

Though they differ on the amount of money required, Congress and the administration clearly are determined to commit new resources to technological and scientific literacy. Adult literacy advocates wish the same could be said for their cause.

Selected Bibliography

Books

Copperman, Paul, *The Literacy Hoax*, Morrow, 1978.

Flesch, Rudolf, *Why Johnny Still Can't Read*, Harper & Row, 1981.

Hunter, Carman St. John and Harman, David, *Adult Illiteracy in the United States*, McGraw-Hill, 1979.

Kozol, Jonathan, *Prisoners of Silence,* Continuum, 1980.

Maeroff, Gene I., *Don't Blame the Kids*, McGraw-Hill, 1982.

Smith, Edwin H., *Literacy Education for Adolescents and Adults*, Boyd & Fraser, 1970

Articles

"A Nation of Illiterates?" *U.S. News & World Report*, May 17, 1982.

"Athletes' Test Scores," *The New York Times*, Jan. 14, 1983.

"Adult Illiteracy in the United States," *National Association for Public Continuing and Adult Education Exchange*, Summer 1980.

"Teaching to Think: A New Emphasis," Education Winter Survey, *The New York Times,* Jan. 9, 1983.

"The Secret Handicap: Millions of American Adults Can't Read" (first of three parts), *The Washington Post*, Nov. 25, 1982.

Reports and Studies

Center for Public Resources, "Basic Skills in the U.S. Work Force," November 1982.

Editorial Research Reports: "Education's Return to Basics," 1975 Vol. II, p. 667; "Competency Tests," 1978 Vol. II, p. 603.

Feistritzer Publications, "The American Teacher," 1983.

National Assessment of Educational Progress *Newsletter,* "Graduates May Lack Tomorrow's 'Basics,' " fall 1982.

——"Reading, Science and Mathematics Trends, A Closer Look," December 1982.

——"Action for Excellence," June 1983.

National Commission on Excellence in Education, "A Nation At Risk: The Imperative for Educational Reform," April 1983.

National Institute of Education, "The Adult Illiterate Speaks Out: Personal Perspectives on Learning to Read and Write," September 1980.

University of Texas at Austin, "Adult Functional Competency: A Summary," March 1975.

Graphics: Cover illustration by Staff Artist Robert Redding; p. 93 cartoon by Sidney Harris; pp. 97, 100 illustrations by George Rebh.

SCHOOLBOOK CONTROVERSIES

by

William Sweet

Sept. 10
1 9 8 2

Editor's Note: Since this report was written, the plaintiffs in *Grove v. Mead School District No. 354* lost in federal district court and are appealing to the 9th Circuit Court of Appeals.

SCHOOLBOOK CONTROVERSIES

O N SEPT. 21, a case is scheduled to go to trial in Spokane, Wash., in which the plaintiffs are asking for a permanent injunction against the use in school of *The Learning Tree,* an autobiographical novel by Gordon Parks describing the experiences of a black man struggling in white society. The case may not go far, but it is worthy of note because it has so much in common with other actions against books that are being brought by students, parents and teachers in school districts around the country. The cases are testing the novel question of whether school boards and teachers have to take the rights of children and teen-age students into account when assigning reading or stocking libraries.

In a typical dispute, both opponents and defenders of books argue that their constitutional rights are threatened.[1] Each side, supported by phalanxes of lawyers, accuses the other of trying to exercise censorship or purvey propaganda. As students return to school this fall, many will find battles of this kind raging around them. What they read in class or in the library will depend on how these political battles are resolved at school board meetings or in the courts.

The Learning Tree suit, *Grove v. Mead School District No. 354,* was filed in December 1980 by an attorney for the Moral Majority of Washington Legal Foundation on behalf of parents, who had tried without success to persuade the Mead School District in suburban Spokane to ban the use of the book in courses. The plaintiffs complain that the book contains obscenities, explicit sexual material and blasphemies against Jesus Christ, and they say it purveys "the anti-God religion of humanism which is antithetical to plaintiffs' beliefs and which violates the free exercise and no establishment clauses" of the Constitution. In other words, the plaintiffs argue that assignment of the book in a public school amounts to government promotion of a particular religion and infringes on their right to practice their religion freely.

The Mead County prosecutor's office, which is defending the

---

[1] Both opponents and defenders of individual books have relied on the First Amendment, which says that "Congress shall make no law respecting an establishment of religion, or prohibiting the free exercise thereof; or abridging the freedom of speech, or of the press...."

local school board, has filed for dismissal of the case on the ground that the plaintiffs have no standing. Of the three parent-plaintiffs, only one has a student in the school, and the student is not a party to the suit. The Washington Education Association, the state affiliate of the National Education Association, has filed a brief taking issue with the plaintiffs' argument that their constitutional rights are being violated. The Washington state branch of the American Civil Liberties Union has filed an amicus brief that is favorable to the defense.

U.S. District Court Judge Robert McNichols is scheduled to hold a hearing to consider pretrial briefs on Sept. 13, and he may well issue a summary judgment dismissing the case. On the face of it, the school board can make a strong case that it has followed proper procedures and given the plaintiffs a fair hearing. It appointed a review panel to consider the complaint, held public hearings and finally gave students who objected to *The Learning Tree* the option of reading another book.

For these reasons, the defense attorneys consider dismissal of the suit probable. On the other hand, a recent Supreme Court decision, in which the justices ordered a somewhat similar suit remanded to a lower court for trial *(see p. 115)*, could encourage Judge McNichols to hold a trial for the sake of developing a complete factual record. Because the legal questions raised by challenges to schoolbooks are new and untested, there is something to be said for exploring individual cases in some depth.

Teachers and parents traditionally have decided what is discussed in schools and how it is discussed. The notion that students have First Amendment rights to read certain writings is relatively new. If students do have such rights, how far do they extend and how should they be protected? Do students have a right to obtain, in courses or school libraries, any materials relevant to educational topics, even when the materials are readily available in bookstores or public libraries?

If students do have a right to see such material in school, does this imply that schools have an obligation to provide it? Are there legitimate reasons for removing books from schools, and if so, how are they to be distinguished from illegitimate reasons? Should schools be obliged to present points of view favored by individual religious or political sects, regardless of how unreasonable such perspectives may seem to most parents and educators? These are some of the key questions raised in a large number of recent controversies over schoolbooks.

Number and Nature of Schoolbook Fights

According to the American Library Association's Office for Intellectual Freedom, complaints about library books increased

from about 300 in 1979-80 to between 900 and 1,000 in 1980-81. While statistics for 1981-82 have yet to be compiled, the ALA expects the number to be about the same. Between 70 and 80 percent of the complaints have concerned school library books. Most of the remainder involved books in public or small college libraries.

In 1980, the ALA undertook, in conjunction with the Association of American Publishers and the Association for Supervision and Curriculum Development, a survey of schoolbook complaints. Nearly 1,900 librarians, principals and superintendents responded to the mail and telephone poll. More than one-fifth of them reported that there had been some kind of challenge to classroom or library materials since Sept. 1, 1978.[2]

Complaints about sex, obscenity and profanity were involved in nearly half the challenges. Other prevalent reasons for challenges concerned alleged religious or racial bias, undermining the "traditional family values," excessively critical views of U.S. history, the teaching of Darwin's evolutionary theory without

[2] See AAP, ALA and ASCD, "Limiting What Students Shall Read" (1981), p. 3. Survey available from Association of American Publishers, 2005 Massachusetts Ave., N.W., Washington, D.C. 20036.

reference to the biblical account of creation, and "values clari-
fication" approaches to teaching — a method that encourages
students to formulate and refine their own values, regardless of
whether they are consistent with prevailing religious or moral
standards.

The survey found that more than three quarters of the challenges to the books came from individuals speaking just for
themselves, and about 30 percent from school staff members.
Teachers, librarians and administrators opposed challenges in
six out of every 10 cases they became involved in. Of some 500
challenges specified by respondents to the survey, "some degree
of restriction or censorship was ultimately imposed" in more
than half the cases. More than 90 percent of the time, "the
publisher, producer and/or author were not given an opportunity to defend the challenged material," and in nearly half the
cases "no one was assigned to re-evaluate the challenged
material."

Only about half of the 1,295 responding administrators reported that their schools or districts had formal, written procedures for dealing with challenges. Those districts that did not
have formal policies "more often reported that challenges were
dealt with informally and more often reported that challenged
materials were altered, restricted or removed prior to a formal
review." When challenges were dealt with informally by districts without written procedures, materials ultimately were
removed or restricted more than two-thirds of the time.[3]

Responsibilities of Educators and Parents

The organizations that sponsored the survey of schoolbook
challenges did not deny that parents have a legitimate role in
the selection of reading material for students. Nor did they
claim that challenges necessarily constitute "a threat to freedom
of speech or the ability of our schools to provide quality education." On the contrary, they affirmed that challenges have a
proper place in a "democratic educational system." What the
sponsors found disturbing was the overwhelming tendency of
challenges to limit rather than expand reading material and,
above all, the restriction or censorship of material without formal procedure.

While the sponsors willingly recognize the legitimate role of
parents in selecting books, they believe that other competent
parties should have an opportunity to make their views known
as well. The American Library Association takes the position
that libraries have a responsibility to provide full access to a
wide range of information and ideas, including views that may

[3] *Ibid.,* pp. 6, 8.

Representative Sample
of Challenged School Materials

Author or Sponsor	Work
	American Heritage Dictionary, 1969 ed.
Bannerman, Helen	*Little Black Sambo*
Berrigan, Daniel	*Trial of the Catonsville Nine*
Brown, Claude	*Manchild in the Promised Land*
Ebony magazine	"Ray Charles' Sex Life"
Fromm, Erich	*The Art of Loving*
Govt. of South Africa	"South Africa" (film)
Hawthorne, Nathaniel	*The Scarlet Letter*
Hentoff, Nat	*This School Is Driving Me Crazy*
Huxley, Aldous	*Brave New World*
Kerr, M. E.	*Dinky Hocker Shoots Smack*
Nilsson, Lennart	*How Was I Born? A Photographic Story of Reproduction ...*
Roth, Philip	*Portnoy's Complaint*
Sendak, Maurice	*Where the Wild Things Are*
Shakespeare, William	*The Merchant of Venice*
Staurianos, L. S.	"Man the Toolmaker" (film)

be unorthodox and unpopular in the local community. The doctrine of full access to information is enshrined in a "library bill of rights," which the ALA adopted in 1948.

The National Education Association and the American Federation of Teachers, like the ALA, encourage their members to assert themselves in the book-selection process. Teachers, like librarians, take it for granted that it is part of their job to identify significant materials for use in school. The National Association of High School Principals, on the other hand, emphatically backs the right of school boards to act as the ultimate arbiters of what students should see.

Ivan Gluckman, legal counsel to the principals' association, conceded in an interview that librarians should try to stock materials expressing a wide range of views. But "if librarians think it's part of their job to decide what pupils should read," he said, "they're wrong." He said that the ideal of academic freedom, in which the immunity of educational institutions from political pressures is held sacred, "applies mainly at the college level, where the pursuit of pure knowledge is at stake," not in primary or secondary schools.[4]

Among the people who have defended the right of school boards to bar books from school libraries and courses is Dr. Terrel H. Bell, the U.S. secretary of education. In an interview with the Baltimore *Sun*, Bell said that since school attendance

[4] Interview, Aug. 9, 1982.

is generally mandatory, students should not be forced to read "literature that may be objectionable and would insult the sensibilities and the values of the home." [5] In 1974, as commissioner of education in the Ford administration, Bell defended parents and fundamentalist preachers who protested books being used in Kanawha County, W.Va., public schools. Among the objectionable books were some by black writers critical of whites, anti-war poetry and a Mark Twain satire on the Book of Genesis.[6]

As a Mormon and as a father of a large family, Bell is sympathetic to communities that have a special view of religious and domestic values, but as the author of five education books and a novel, he also places great value on freedom to read and write. In interviews and speeches, Bell has distinguished between optional and required reading. Apparently he believes that students should be able to read what they want in elective courses, provided their parents do not object. But in required courses, he thinks students should have "freedom from speech" as well as "freedom of speech."[7] The books he would scratch from required reading lists, in deference to community values, include novels by William Faulkner, James Joyce and Ernest Hemingway, Chaucer's *Canterbury Tales,* Kurt Vonnegut Jr.'s *Slaughterhouse Five,* William Golding's *Lord of the Flies* and J. D. Salinger's *The Catcher in the Rye.*

Books and Groups in Dispute

THE BOOKS and authors most often banned from school reading are easy enough to identify *(see box, p. 111).* It is not always so easy to tell, though, exactly why they are banned. For example, *The Catcher in the Rye* is one of the books most frequently barred from libraries and courses, ostensibly because of its sexually provocative language, but probably also because of its alienated and irreverent attitude toward the adult world. *Slaughterhouse Five* also crops up repeatedly in book controversies for a mixture of reasons. Parents and teachers often object to its raunchy language, but at bottom, they may be more concerned about the critical views it expresses of U.S. conduct in World War II.[8]

---

[5] *The Sun,* March 28, 1981.

[6] A parent's suit against the Kanawha Board of Education drew a ruling by U.S. District Court Judge Kenneth H. Hall, Jan. 30, 1975, that while the books might be offensive to the plaintiffs' beliefs, they did not violate the principle of separation of church and state.

[7] Quoted in *The Christian Science Monitor,* March 24, 1981.

[8] *Slaughterhouse Five* is about the fire bombing of Dresden, Germany, in 1945. About 100,000 civilians died as the result of U.S.-British air raids for which there appeared to be no compelling military reason.

An orderly process of meetings and public discussion can shed light on the precise motives for book complaints and open the way for resolution of conflicts. When political or religious objections turn out to have been cloaked in complaints about language or style, a majority of the community may decide to overrule the objections. Sometimes complaints turn out to be based on misunderstandings or exaggerated first impressions.

Earlier this year, the principal of Mark Twain Intermediate School in Fairfax County, Va., recommended that Twain's *The Adventures of Huckleberry Finn* be removed from the curriculum. The principal acted on the recommendation of a racially mixed panel that objected to "the flagrant use of the word 'nigger' and the demeaning way in which black people are portrayed in the book." A Fairfax County superintendent refused to accept the principal's recommendation, and after a number of newspaper columnists patiently explained that criticism of slavery and racism was a theme of the book, the high school committee reversed its position and accepted the book for use in the curriculum.

When objections to a book are based on just a few words or passages, disputes sometimes can be resolved by editing the offending material or replacing the book with a similar one. Parents, teachers and librarians often complain about dictionaries with definitions of "dirty" words. While this may strike some liberal-minded parents as nit-picking of the worst kind, to librarians who watch adolescents wasting whole afternoons searching for salacious words, it may seem mere common sense to find a less inviting reference work.

The same goes for sex education guides. Many parents do not object to sex education any more than they object to dictionaries, but when it is a question of what their teenage sons and daughters will read in school, they may prefer to replace materials that contain highly explicit illustrations or suggestive prose. At the same time, many parents regard sex education strictly as the responsibility of the family, and they consider any discussion of the subject in school an invitation to premarital sexual activity.[9]

---

[9] See "Sex Education," *E.R.R.*, 1981 Vol. II, pp. 633-652.

Members of groups like the Rev. Jerry Falwell's Moral Majority and Phyllis Schlafly's Eagle Forum tend to regard sex education as just one prong in a national offensive mounted by their adversaries to impose a libertine, anti-family ideology and lifestyle on the country.

The Traditionalists vs. Civil Libertarians

These conservative groups have adopted the term "secular humanism" to describe the beliefs held by their antagonists. They use the term to describe people who reject biblical authority and traditional customs in favor of scientific inquiry and relativistic morality.[10] As the traditionalists see it, much of what passes for biology, social science and history really is propaganda for the secular humanist position. In their eyes, an anthropology book that describes exotic sexual rites in objective terms, without passing express judgment on them, adds up to an endorsement of the view that any custom is just as good as any other. By the same token, a biology text explaining Darwin's theory of evolution amounts to an implicit critique of the Biblical account of creation.

Generally, traditionalist groups reject the charge that they advocate book banning. They insist, to the contrary, that they are merely trying to get equal time for their point of view. Schlafly, based in Alton, Ill., has urged Eagle Forum members to check whether local libraries stock books that oppose the Equal Rights Amendment, which she campaigned against. She has also encouraged members to persuade their libraries to buy certain books that express politically and socially conservative perspectives. The thrust of her schoolbook campaign, which is managed by the Stop Textbook Censorship Committee, is to push for abolition of required reading lists. Schlafly believes they are biased against the traditional role of women.

Activities of such groups have caused alarm among political liberals and civil libertarians, who fear a resurgence of witch hunting. A year ago, prominent figures including television producer Norman Lear and Notre Dame University President Theodore Hesberg founded "People for the American Way," which describes itself as a "nonprofit, nonpartisan, educational organization dedicated to reaffirming and celebrating America's constitutional rights to think, speak and worship freely."

Based in Washington, People for the American Way has launched a National Schools and Libraries Project to counter what its director, Barbara Parker, calls a "nationwide epidemic" of censorship. One of her project's aims is to organize a network of national groups with local units that could involve themselves

---

[10] For background, see "The New Humanism," *E.R.R.*, 1970 Vol. II, pp. 813-832.

in book disputes. Parker believes that the best way to neutralize a "well organized, well financed and [seemingly] well orchestrated" censorship campaign is to assure that communities are as broadly represented as possible in book selection.

People associated with civil libertarian groups tend to portray the opposing groups in almost conspiratorial terms, as is indicated by titles of some recent books describing "New Right" activities.[11] But information circulated by the Committee Against Censorship in New York indicates that the traditionalist groups have been far from omnipotent. Courts in Colorado and Indiana, among others, have affirmed the right of school boards to restrict books even when the decisions are based strictly on the personal, political or moral views of the members. In some other states, however — among them Maine, Massachusetts, Minnesota and New Hampshire — courts have issued rulings in favor of students' "right to read" and to "receive information." [12]

In a widely publicized decison last January, U.S. District Court Judge William R. Overton overturned a 1981 Arkansas state law that required "balanced treatment" — a law that invited attention to the Biblical account of creation in the school. Judge Overton held the law unconstitutional on the ground that it required biology teachers to propagate religious doctrine. His opinion reflected the consensus of scientists and biology teachers that the story of how the world was created in the book of Genesis is not a scientific theory on a par with Darwinism.[13]

Supreme Court Ruling in New York Case

Last June, the Supreme Court handed down its first decision ever in a case involving the right of public school students to retain reading material found objectionable by the community. The case, *Island Trees Board of Education v. Pico,* arose from a complaint members of a group called Parents of New York United (PONY-U) brought against the school board over nine books in a Long Island school library.[14]

The school board appointed a committee of educators and parents to investigate the complaints, but after the committee recommended retention of the books, the board decided to

---

[11] For example, *Holy Terror: The Fundamentalist War on America's Freedoms in Religion, Politics and Our Private Lives* (1982) by Flo Conway and Jim Siegelman, and *The New Subversives: Anti-Americanism of the Religious Right* (1982) by Daniel C. Maguire.
[12] See National Coalition Against Censorship, *Censorship News*, March 1982 and May 1982.
[13] See Allen Hammon and Lynn Margulis, "Creationism as Science," *Science81*, December 1981, pp. 55-61.
[14] The books were *Soul on Ice* by Eldridge Cleaver; *A Hero Ain't Nothing But a Sandwich* by Alice Childress; *The Fixer* by Bernard Malamud; *Go Ask Alice,* anonymous; *Slaughterhouse Five* by Kurt Vonnegut Jr.; *The Best Short Stories by Negro Writers,* ed. by Langston Hughes; *Black Boy* by Richard Wright; *Laughing Boy* by Oliver LaFarge; and *The Naked Ape* by Desmond Morris.

remove them anyway, characterizing them as "anti-American, anti-Christian and just plain filthy." Students took the case to the federal district court, which issued a summary judgment in favor of the school board. The Second U.S. Circuit Court of Appeals (for New York) reversed the lower court's decision and remanded the case for trial. By a fragmented 5-4 decision, the Supreme Court on June 25 upheld the decision of the appeals court.

Justice Brennan announced the court's decison and delivered an opinion in which Justices Stevens and Marshall joined in full, and Justice Blackmun in part. Justice White concurred in the court's decision, but considered it unnecessary before the case was tried to deliver "a dissertation on the extent to which the First Amendment limits the discretion of the school board to remove books from the school library." Chief Justice Burger wrote the dissenting opinion, joined by Justices Powell, Rehnquist and O'Connor, all of whom wrote additional opinions of their own.

Justice Brennan opened his opinion by enunciating the principle that students do not "shed their rights to freedom of speech or expression at the schoolhouse gate," and he argued that the right to free expression implies a "right to receive information." He said the right applied especially to the school library, where "a regime of voluntary inquiry" holds sway, as opposed to "the compulsory environment of the classroom." Emphasizing that his decision applied only to the removal of books and only to school libraries, Brennan granted school boards "significant discretion" but said they must not exercise that discretion "in a narrowly partisan or political manner."

Justice Blackmun, in a concurring opinion, did not accept Brennan's distinction between class and library or his argument about the "right to receive information." But he too said that "school officials may not remove books for the purpose of restricting access to the political ideas or social perspectives discussed in them, when that action is motivated simply by the officials' disapproval of the ideas involved."

Chief Justice Burger agreed with Brennan that students do not shed their right to free speech at the gate, but said that removal of books from the school library in no way abridges that right, since the books can be obtained at public libraries or bookstores. He argued that there is no way to determine what is a partisan motive for removing a book without making a partisan judgment. He found the distinction between acquisition and removal of books spurious and rejected the notion that "the Constitution requires school boards to justify to its [sic] teenage pupils the decision to remove a particular book."

Justice Powell stressed that "school boards are uniquely local and democratic institutions," and he said the court's decision "symbolizes a debilitating encroachment upon the institutions of a free people." Justice Rehnquist argued that students have the right only to information deemed appropriate by their educators. "Education consists of the selective presentation and explanation of ideas," he said. "The effective acquisition of knowledge depends upon an orderly exposure to relevant information."

Justice O'Connor, in the court's most concise opinion, said that if a school board can choose curriculum, teachers and what books to purchase initially for a library, "it surely can decide which books to discontinue ... so long as it does not also interfere with the right of students to read the material and discuss it."

Politics of Textbook Selection

WHETHER the complicated and ambivalent Supreme Court decision in *Island Trees* will provide adequate guidance to lower courts remains to be seen. The high court sought to distinguish between legitimate and illegitimate motives for banning books from school. By implication, the presence of sexually provocative material or the absence of worthy educational ideas might provide sound grounds for excluding books, but purely political motives would not. In practice, though, it may be difficult, as several dissenting justices argued, to make a sharp distinction between political and non-political motives.

All of the books that figured in the *Island Trees* case contain obscenities or sexually explicit material. Coincidentally or not, eight of them were by or about members of ethnic minority groups, and the ninth — *The Naked Ape* — is based on Darwinian concepts. The more objectionable passages could be excised in a compromise solution, but that would only draw attention to them, and it is not always clear how much material could be deleted without doing serious damage to the content of the books.

In Eldridge Cleaver's *Soul on Ice,* for example, some of the provocative passages can be interpreted as an integral part of his critique of white society. In much of modern literature, and especially in works by members of ethnic minorities or working class groups, sex is used as a weapon in quasi-political attacks on the dominant white Protestant culture, which is often portrayed as repressive and uptight. Parents may argue that the critical perspectives in such books can be understood without the sex, but the authors evidently did not think so, or they would not have dealt with sexual relations in the first place.

1960s Revolution in Social Science Texts

According to *America Revised,* a collection of essays by Francis FitzGerald on U.S. history textbooks, public protests against texts occurred as early as the mid-19th century. They "grew in size and intensity with the establishment of universal secondary education, in the twentieth." The first really big burst of book challenges took place after World War I, when the isolationist press attacked the pro-British bias of certain texts.[15] In the midst of this controversy, Henry Steele Commager — the distinguished author of several leading history texts — was persuaded to modify his account of the Bunker Hill battle as follows: "Three times the British returned courageously to the attack," the original read; "Three times the cowardly British returned to the attack," read the revised version.

Partly because of the absence of a strong intellectual tradition in secondary education, and partly because of the emphasis put on training in civic virtue, the textbook selection process has always tended to be quite political in the United States. One of the most famous textbook battles erupted on the eve of World War II over a series on American civilization by Dr. Harold Rugg. The series, which discussed sensitive issues like unemployment, immigrants' problems, class structure, central planning and socialism, was quite popular during the Depression years.

But in 1939, when a conservative coalition was beginning to outflank the New Deal's supporters, the Advertising Federation of America, the National Association of Manufacturers, the American Legion and several other organizations launched an attack on the series because of its left-liberal perspectives. In 1938, the Rugg's books sold nearly 300,000 copies; in 1944, sales dropped to 21,000, and shortly thereafter, the book disappeared from the market.[16]

For 20 years after World War II, when the United States was locked in a cold war with what was seen as a monolithic world communist threat, almost all American social science texts presented a laudatory version of U.S. history and society. In school, if not in the poetry and novels written by the "beat generation," the United States was described as a land of freedom and opportunity, and as a uniquely stable and peace-loving nation

---

[15] Francis FitzGerald, *America Revised* (1979), p. 35.
[16] *Ibid.,* p. 37.

The Scopes Trial

This, the most famous of school controversies, arose in the 1920s out of a conflict between religious traditionalists, who called themselves Fundamentalists, and Modernists or religious liberals. The Fundamentalists refused to accept the validity of scientific teachings that conflicted with a literal interpretation of the Bible, while the Modernists sought to reconcile the Bible with contemporary science. The Fundamentalists introduced bills in nearly half of the state legislatures to forbid the teaching of evolution, and in Tennessee, Oklahoma and Mississippi they succeeded in getting the legislation enacted.

In the small town of Dayton, Tenn., a young mining engineer named George Rappelyea persuaded a friend, John Thomas Scopes, to test the new law by deliberately teaching the doctrine of evolution to a public school student. Scopes took up the challenge and was arrested. William Jennings Bryan, who had run for president three times and served as President Wilson's secretary of state, volunteered his services to the prosecution. Clarence Darrow, the famous lawyer known for his defense of radicals and underdog causes, represented Scopes with the assistance of two other attorneys.

The trial, in July 1925, turned into a media event and ended with a dramatic confrontation between Bryan and Darrow, in which the aging statesman was subjected to a humiliating cross-examination about his religious beliefs. Bryan died five days later. Scopes was convicted and fined $100, but the state Supreme Court later cleared him on a technicality, though it upheld the anti-evolution law.

In the estimation of Federick Lewis Allen, the author of *Only Yesterday* (1931), "there was something to be said for the right of the people to decide what should be taught in their tax-supported schools, even if what they decided upon was ridiculous. But the issue of the Scopes case, as the great mass of newspaper readers saw it, was nothing so abstruse as the rights of taxpayers versus academic freedom. In the eyes of the public, the trial was a battle betwen Fundamentalists on the one hand and twentieth-century skepticism (assisted by Modernism) on the other."

— a country which fought only when forced to and only when the cause was just, and which always won when it did fight. This was the orthodox view until the late 1960s, when the civil rights movement and a reaction against the Vietnam War produced a revolution in social science texts.

Leftists and minority groups loudly protested that the traditional history texts had ignored or unfairly portrayed the minorities and given American history a self-congratulatory view.[17] After a period of reappraisal and revision, the emphasis switched. There were accounts of a country with a bundle of

---

[17] See "American History: Reappraisal and Revision," *E.R.R.*, 1969 Vol. II, pp. 815-834.

unsolved problems and a history of distasteful episodes — Indian massacres, enslavement of blacks, exploitation of immigrants and imperialist wars. The story of the dominant European groups was no longer the whole story, and their contributions to the United States were no longer seen as unequivocally praiseworthy.

Mustering for Battle in 'Adoption States'

It was in reaction to the 1960s revolution that groups like Schlafly's Eagle Forum and the Pro-Family Forum in Fort Worth, Texas, entered the schoolbook fray. Increasingly, the so-called "adoption states" have emerged as the main arena for combat between the traditionalists and the book reformers. In some 22 states, central committees meet annually to review new textbooks submitted by publishers for use in primary and secondary schools. In some of these states, the committees issue relatively loose recommendations or guidelines to be followed by local boards, while in others the committees decide in very specific terms what can and cannot be bought.[18]

Texas, because of its size and its exceptionally strict selection procedures, is the most important of the adoption states. School boards in Texas are expected to spend about $60 million this year on textbooks — all "adopted" by the State Textbook Committee. Lured by this lucrative market, publishers are thought to take Texas' preferences — specifically the committee's preferences — heavily into account when they design books. "It would be very difficult to write off the Texas market," said William Wood, Texas representative of the Follett Publishing Company.[19]

The traditionalist groups rely heavily in Texas on the work of Mel and Norma Gabler, a couple in Longview who have been systematically scouring textbooks for more than two decades. This year, of roughly 900 pages of objections submitted to Texas' State Textbook Committee, about 600 came from the Gablers' organization, Educational Research Analysts. People for the American Way has opened a Texas Project to counter the influence of the Gablers, and at the end of July, the project received permission from the textbook committee to file rejoinders to objections.[20]

---

[18] The adoption states are Alabama, Arkansas, California, Florida, Georgia, Hawaii, Indiana, Kentucky, Louisiana, Mississippi, Nevada, New Mexico, North Carolina, Oklahoma, Oregon, South Carolina, Tennessee, Texas, Utah, Virginia, Washington and West Virginia. Procedures vary widely from state to state. Statewide adoption in California, for example, applies only to elementary school texts.

[19] Quoted by Barbara Parker, in a letter published in *The Washington Post*, Aug. 28, 1982.

[20] The textbook committee met in early September to consider books, complaints and rejoinders. The State Board of Education is scheduled to meet Nov. 13 to make final decisions about textbooks.

Schoolbooks in Context

DEMOCRATIC procedures, for all their virtues, can and often do produce ludicrous results. Maybe this is why authors sometimes react with an amused shrug when they hear that their books have been banned by local communities. When *Huckleberry Finn* was first published in 1885, it was widely attacked as coarse and degenerate, and a number of communities including Concord, Mass., barred it from their libraries. Twain found it ironic, or so he claimed, that communities would ban his book while continuing to encourage children to read the Bible, a book filed with stories about sinful behavior. "The truth is," Twain said, "that when a library expels a book of mine and leaves an unexpurgated Bible around where unprotected youth and age can get hold of it, the deep unconscious irony of it delights me and doesn't anger me." [21]

Ken Kesey reacted in much the same spirit when he heard that his book *One Flew Over the Cuckoo's Nest* had become the subject of a high school fight in St. Anthony, Idaho. Kesey wrote a letter to the students and educators saying, "I object to 'Cuckoo's Nest' being taught. What's there to teach? It's an entirely simple work, a book that any high school kid can read and comprehend without help. Let 'Cuckoo's Nest' alone on the drugstore rack and teach instead 'Moby Dick' . . . for crying out loud." [22]

Not every author takes the news of a book banning lying down. Earlier this year, when parents in Girard, Pa., objected to the assignment of *Working* by Studs Terkel, a book about what it is like to do various blue-collar and white-collar jobs in the United States, Terkel went to the working-class town near Erie to defend his work. In March, the Girard school board unanimously refused to withdraw the book or permit assignment of other reading to students who objected to its coarse language.

Recent Limits on Information and Expression

Since World War II, the general trend had been toward significantly greater freedom of expression and more access to information in the United States. Important landmarks have included:

> **On obscenity,** the Supreme Court's 1957 decision in *Roth v. United States, Alberts v. California,* in which Justice Brennan wrote that works with "even the slightest redeeming social importance" shall have full protection under the Constitution, even when they are "hateful to the prevailing climate of opinion."

---

[21] Quoted by Haynes Johnson in *The Washington Post,* April 11, 1982.
[22] Quoted by Noel Epstein in *The Washington Post,* March 14, 1982.

On access to government data, the enactment in 1966 of the Freedom of Information Act, which require the federal government to make documents available to citizens upon request; and the expansion of the act in 1974 legislation.

On national security, the Supreme Court's 1971 decision in *New York Times Company v. United States,* in which the court refused to grant the government an injunction against publication in the *Times* of the "Pentagon Papers," excerpts from official documents that showed how the United States got involved in the Vietnam war.[23]

In recent years, however, the trend has been toward a somewhat more restrictive attitude toward information. The Supreme Court, in *Miller v. California* (1973), retreated from Brennan's 1957 definition of obscenity and made it easier for states to ban material considered sexually offensive.[24] During the late 1970s, after the nation's reaction against the Vietnam War began to wear off, the government started to reassert its authority to keep certain types of national security information confidential.

In 1979, the Carter administration sought an unprecedented court injunction, under authority of the Atomic Energy Act of 1954, to prevent publication in *The Progressive* magazine of an article on "how to build a hydrogen bomb." The case became moot when a newspaper published essentially the same material, but the restrictive 1954 law remains on the books.[25] The Carter administration also sought to prevent publication of books about Central Intelligence Agency activities written by former agents, in violation of written agreements they had made with the agency. The Carter White House issued guidelines that gave the CIA somewhat greater latitude to conduct secret operations.[26]

Since President Reagan took office, the CIA has been given an even longer leash. This year, Congress passed a "names of agents" bill that makes it a crime to publish the identities of U.S. secret agents even when the information is obtained from public documents.[27] In April, Reagan issued an executive order making it considerably easier for the government to classify material. Administration officials, most notably Adm. Bobby Inman, the former deputy director of the CIA, have warned repeatedly that it may be necessary to impose restrictions on the publication of scientific information that might be helpful

---

[23] For background on the case, see "Secrecy in Government," *E.R.R.,* 1971 Vol. II, pp. 627-650.

[24] See "Pornography Business Upsurge," *E.R.R.,* 1979 Vol. II, pp. 765-780.

[25] See "Atomic Secrecy," *E.R.R.,* 1979 Vol. II, pp. 641-659.

[26] See "Intelligence Agencies Under Fire," *E.R.R.,* 1979 Vol. II, pp. 941-962.

[27] See *Congressional Quarterly Weekly Report,* June 19, 1982, p. 1490.

to adversary nations like Russia. The administration has been trying to get scientists to exercise self-censorship with regard to sensitive scientific and technological advances.[28]

In 1981 the administration attempted to bar publications from Cuba under authority of the 1962 Trading with the Enemy Act, but after coming under wide attack in the press, the administration relented. It now permits individuals to freely import written materials from Cuba. Last December, however, FBI agents seized 11 books from journalists who were returning to the United States from Iran. The books, which are readily available in other countries, purportedly contain information on U.S. activities in Iran prior to its revolution. The journalists, represented by the ACLU, have sued the FBI and the U.S. Customs Service.[29]

Writers have become especially concerned during the past couple of years about a growing number of libel suits in which the plaintiffs have won large cash judgments. It is feared that the suits are having a chilling effect on newspaper and book publishers. In a series of decisions during the 1960s, starting with *The New York Times Co. v. Sullivan,* the Supreme Court held that public officials and public figures could not recover damages for libel unless actual malice could be shown. During the 1970s, however, the Supreme Court has tended to narrow the definition of a public figure and widen the scope for libel.[30]

For all that, the United States remains, even by comparison with the democratic countries of Western Europe, one of the world's most free countries as far as freedom of expression and access to information are concerned. Congress repeatedly has rejected proposals for an "official secrets act," to be modeled on English legislation.

While the scope of free inquiry has perhaps become somewhat more restricted during the past decade in the United States, it would be a mistake to interpret the current wave of schoolbook banning as a retreat from some mythical golden age when students supposedly had complete freedom of speech. It is, in fact, only in response to the wave of book challenges that courts have guaranteed, for the first time, a right for school students to see certain materials or at least not be deprived of them. Ironically, the final result of the schoolbook controversies may be that students will have their First Amendment rights more firmly secured, albeit within certain boundaries.

[28] See "Controlling Scientific Information," *E.R.R.*, 1982 Vol. II, pp. 489-508.
[29] See National Coalition Against Censorship, *Censorship News,* March 1982, p. 7.
[30] See "High Cost of Libel," *E.R.R.*, 1981 Vol. II, pp. 769-788.

Selected Bibliography

Books

FitzGerald, Francis, *America Revised: History Schoolbooks in the Twentieth Century,* Little, Brown and Co., 1979.

Hofstadter, Richard, *Anti-Intellectualism in American Life,* Alfred A. Knopf, 1964.

Jenkinson, Edward B., *Censors in the Classroom: The Mind Benders,* University of Illinois Press, 1979.

Articles

Arons, Stephen, "Book Burning in the Heartland," *Saturday Review,* July 21, 1979.

——"The Crusade to Ban Books," *Saturday Review,* June 1981.

Dahlin, Robert, "A Tough Time for Textbooks," *Publishers Weekly,* Aug. 7, 1981.

Hegstad, Roland R., "More Bodies," *Liberty,* January-February 1982.

Krauthammer, Charles, "The Humanist Phantom," *The New Republic,* July 25, 1981.

Nelkin, Dorothy, "The Science Textbook Controversies," *Scientific American,* April 1976.

Nocera, Joseph, "The Big Book-Banning Brawl," *The New Republic,* Sept. 13, 1982.

Skow, John, Allen Hammond and Lynn Margulis, "The Creationists," *Science81,* December 1981.

Weissman, Arnie, "Building the Tower of Babel," *Texas Outlook,* winter 1981-82.

Reports and Studies

Association of American Publishers, the American Library Association and the Association for Supervision and Curriculum Development, "Limiting What Students Shall Read," Washington, D.C., 1981.

Donelson, Kenneth L., "The Students' Right to Read," National Council of Teachers of English, Urbana, Ill., 1972.

Editorial Research Reports: "Changes in Moral Customs and Laws," 1965 Vol. II, p. 499; "American History: Reappraisal and Revision," 1969 Vol. II, p. 815; "Book Publishing," 1975 Vol. II, p. 327.

Cover art by Staff Artist Robert Redding;
cartoon on p. 109 by Ben Sargent.

SCHOOL PRAYER

by

Roger Thompson

Sept. 16
1 9 8 3

Editor's Note: Since this report was published Congress, on July 25, 1984, cleared for the president legislation permitting religious groups to meet in schools before and after classes. The measure makes it unlawful for any high school receiving federal funds to deny the use of its buildings to religious, political and other student groups for voluntary meetings before or after school if it allows such access to other extracurricular groups.

The House July 26 also approved a measure to require schools to allow silent prayer in the classroom. Final resolution of that legislation was pending at the time this book went to press.

SCHOOL PRAYER

EIGHT OUT of every 10 Americans believe public school students should be allowed to engage in voluntary prayer, a belief incorporated into the 1980 Republican Party platform and championed by President Reagan in the form of a proposed constitutional amendment.[1] The amendment is scheduled to come to a vote in the Senate this fall.[2] Its effect, says Reagan, would be to "remove the bar to school prayer established by the Supreme Court and allow prayer back in our schools."

The simplicity of Reagan's pitch belies the controversy that has accompanied the school prayer issue for two decades. Teachers and school administrators, the people who would carry out the amendment's intent, tend to oppose it.[3] Most mainline Protestant churches object. Even conservative Protestants represented by the National Association of Evangelicals oppose the amendment, as do Orthodox and Reform Jews. They all support the Supreme Court's 1962 school prayer decision, *Engel v. Vitale (see box, p. 136)*. The Catholic church also opposes the president's amendment, but for a different reason. The church contends it doesn't go far enough. In addition to prayers in schools, it wants voluntary religious instruction.

Primary support comes from fundamentalist Protestant groups such as the Christian Broadcasting Network and the National Christian Action Coalition, and conservative political organizations such as the Rev. Jerry Falwell's Moral Majority, Howard Phillips' Conservative Caucus and Phyllis Schlafly's Eagle Forum. But while school prayer clearly is a conservative issue, some conservatives in the presidents's own party do not support his amendment. In fact, two conservative senators have introduced competing measures with narrower objectives. Sen. Orrin G. Hatch, R-Utah, has proposed a constitutional amend-

---

[1] A Sept. 8, 1983, Gallup Poll indicated that 81 percent of the Americans who had followed the prayer debate favored the proposed amendment; 14 percent opposed it.

[2] Amendments to the Constitution — if not put forward in a constitutional convention — must receive a two-thirds vote in the Senate and House, then approval of three-fourths of the states before becoming law.

[3] The National Education Association, the American Federation of Teachers and the American Association of School Administrators all oppose the president's amendment.

[4] A year later, the court affirmed its school prayer decision, declaring unconstitutional the practice of daily Bible readings in public school classrooms. The 1963 decision covered two separate cases, *School District of Abington Township v. Schempp* and *Murray v. Curlett*.

ment allowing silent prayer or meditation, and student-run school prayer groups. Sen. Jeremiah Denton, R-Ala., has put forth a bill that would deny federal aid to school districts that did not allow students to meet at school facilities for religious purposes. Sen. Mark O. Hatfield, R-Ore., has proposed a similar measure *(see p. 140)*.

With conservatives divided, prospects for success of the president's amendment are dim, concedes Dick Dingman, legislative director of the Moral Majority. "With the Hatch bill waiting, I feel the president's bill is doomed," he said.[5] While Hatch's bill may play a spoiler role, it appears to have no chance of passage this year. Conservatives argue that it is too weak. "We haven't fought all these years for the right to remain silent," said Dingman, who reflects the consensus of the president's supporters.

Defeat for the prayer amendment would leave the president batting zero on his legislative social agenda. An administration bill to ban school busing to overcome racial segregation passed the Senate last year but died in the House. An administration bill to overturn the Supreme Court's 1973 ruling legalizing abortion succumbed to a filibuster in the Senate last year. Although the measure was reintroduced, it was decisively rejected by the Senate on June 28. Reagan's tuition-tax-credit bill to aid parents who send their children to private schools also died in the Senate last session, but has been reintroduced.[6]

What may have a chance at Senate approval is some form of the so-called "religious free speech" legislation offered by Sens. Hatfield and Denton *(see p. 139)*. The Senate Judiciary Committee has yet to act on the proposals. But the free-speech issue is gaining support from a broad spectrum of religious and political groups and could take center stage in the school prayer debate if, as expected, the Reagan and Hatch amendments fail.

Reagan's Commitment to Campaign Promise

Getting prayer back into the public schools was a campaign promise candidate Reagan frequently made to his supporters from the so-called New Right and Religious Right in 1980. The issue, however, took a back seat to economic and defense priorities during Reagan's first 18 months in office. As pressure

---

[5] Interview, Aug. 17, 1983. Persons quoted in the report were interviewed by the author unless otherwise indicated.

[6] It cleared the Senate Finance Committee May 26. The Supreme Court on June 29 gave the bill a boost when it upheld in *Mueller v. Allen* a Minnesota law giving parents a state income tax deduction for the cost of tuition, textbooks and school transportation. The deduction is available to parents with children in public or private schools. The court had disappointed the administration when it upheld by an 8-1 margin on May 24 the Internal Revenue Service's right to deny tax exempt status to racially discriminatory private schools. The administration had argued in *Bob Jones University v. United States* and *Goldsboro Christian Schools v. United States* that the IRS had no such power.

" BOY, DID I GET INTO TROUBLE. I FELL ASLEEP AND HE THOUGHT I WAS PRAYING ! "

mounted for action, Reagan used National Prayer Day, May 6, 1982, to announce his intention to send Congress a constitutional amendment to allow voluntary prayer in the public schools. Reagan noted that religious faith is deeply ingrained in American history: the Pledge of Allegiance declares we are "one nation under God," and our money carries the national motto "In God We Trust." [7] "No one will ever convince me that a moment of voluntary prayer will harm a child or threaten a school or state," Reagan told a White House Rose Garden gathering of religious leaders. The amendment arrived on Capitol Hill 11 days later. It read:

> Nothing in this Constitution shall be construed to prohibit individual or group prayer in the public schools or in other public institutions. No person shall be required by the United States or by any State to participate in prayer.

A White House "fact sheet" attempted to allay fears that the measure would modify the First Amendment's protection of religious freedom. "For 170 years after the adoption of the First Amendment, prayer was permitted in the public schools," it noted, adding the amendment would simply restore the status quo that existed before the Supreme Court's 1962 school prayer decision. Students who do not want to participate in religious exercises would be protected, the fact sheet explained: "Anyone who is offended by the content of any prayer — whether he is a

---

[7] Congress amended the Pledge of Allegiance in 1954, adding the words "under God." Coins have been inscribed with "In God We Trust" since 1864. Congress put the phrase on all currency in 1955; a year later Congress declared it the national motto.

member of a minority religious group, an athiest, or anyone else — can simply refuse to participate; this constitutional right of refusal will be an absolute safeguard against the imposition of sectarian forms of worship."

Administration officials acknowledged that the amendment, as originally proposed, would have allowed state governments to compose school prayers. But Sen. Strom Thurmond, R-S.C., chairman of the Senate Judiciary Committee, changed the wording on July 14 to bar federal or state composition of prayers. However, the measure as amended continues to permit school boards, principals or teachers to select or compose prayers. "The amendment would accept the premise that communities are a more appropriate forum than the federal courts for decisions about the content of school prayers," stated the fact sheet.

The Moral Majority, based in Lynchburg, Va., is in the forefront of lobbying on behalf of the president's amendment. "I don't know of anyone who has been irreparably damaged by the concept of voluntary prayer," said Cal Thomas, the group's vice president for communications. He blamed liberals, led by the American Civil Liberties Union, for "stripping the country of its religious tradition." "The liberals say that even though 75 to 80 percent of the people are for voluntary prayer, they shouldn't have it because it isn't good for them. We say that's a lot of bull. Voluntary prayer is the phalanx that will restore the rights of one of the most persecuted minority groups in this country — those who follow the teachings of Jesus Christ."

Objections to Proposed Prayer Amendment

Opponents of the president's amendment accuse Reagan of playing politics with prayer. They contend that religion was never expelled from the public schools, only government-mandated prayer and Bible readings. Schools may use the Bible or other religious texts as source books for teaching about religion; they may offer a course in the Bible as literature and history; students may pray silently any time they wish; 19 states have adopted laws requiring or permitting schools to observe periods of silence during which students may pray or meditate;[8] students may sing the national anthem and other patriotic songs that contain reference to faith in God; Christmas carols and religious plays are permitted; and school facilities may be rented by religious groups during off-hours if there is a general policy making facilities available to non-school organizations.

[8] The 19 states are Alabama, Arizona, Arkansas, Connecticut, Florida, Georgia, Illinois, Indiana, Kansas, Louisiana, Maine, Maryland, Massachusetts, Michigan, New Jersey, New York, North Dakota, Pennsylvania and Virginia. In New Jersey, however, a federal judge on Jan. 10, 1983, enjoined the state from implementing a law requiring that each school day begin with a one-minute period of silence. The restraining order was still in effect as of Sept. 14.

Religious leaders and constitutional lawyers expressed three major objections to the proposed amendment at hearings before the Senate Judiciary Committee last year. It would, they said, allow government to dictate religious exercises, prescribe sectarian prayers offensive to religious minorities and coerce students to participate in religious exercises under the guise of voluntarism. Professor Paul Bender of the University of Pennsylvania Law School in Philadelphia testified that the amendment would do nothing to limit the kinds of prayers that could be officially adopted: "[The] amendment is drafted to say that 'nothing in this Constitution shall be construed to prohibit prayer in the public schools. . . .' A racist prayer would be perfectly constitutional under this amendment because it says 'nothing in the Constitution' shall prohibit such a prayer." [9]

Others testified that the administration's argument that religious exercises would be voluntary was a constitutional charade. Norman Redlich, dean of the New York University School of Law, echoed the testimony of several witnesses when he said: "Permit school boards, whether in Brooklyn or Utah, to adopt the prayers of the majority, and have Mormon prayers in Utah, and Jewish prayers in New York, then whether they be Catholics or Protestants or Jews, in some parts of the country they will be religious strangers in their own home. There is no way that that cannot be coercive. . . . [I]t is terribly harmful in a matter as personal as religion to have a person be subjected to a religious practice which the majority of the people are able to impose upon the minority. And the fact that you do not tell the person to recite the prayer does not make it any less."

First Amendment Questions

THOSE who push for school prayer take the view that the Supreme Court misinterpreted the intentions of the Founding Fathers who ratified the First Amendment. Professor Grover Rees of the University of Texas Law School in Austin, who assisted the White House staff in drafting the president's amendment, reflected that thought in testimony before the Senate Judiciary Committee on Sept. 16, 1982: "This proposal would make no change at all in the Constitution as it was understood by those who framed and ratified it. Rather, it would have the effect of reversing certain decisions of the U.S. Supreme Court, decisions that seem to have been based on the justices' ideas about what was right for the country rather than

[9] Testifying Aug. 18, 1982.

on their construction of what the Constitution and its amendments meant to those who framed them."

The First Amendment guarantees that "Congress shall make no law respecting an establishiment of religion [the 'establishment clause'], or prohibiting the free exercise thereof [the 'free exercise clause']." There is general agreement that the amendment was intended to prevent Congress from setting up a national church or interfering with religious freedom. Until the mid-20th century, the amendment was generally interpreted as giving the states authority to determine church-state relations within their jurisdictions. In 1947, however, the Supreme Court for the first time ruled that the establishment clause restrictions placed by the First Amendment on the federal government should be applied to state and local governments as well. Not to do so, the Court said in *Everson v. Board of Education*, would allow the states to deprive citizens of religious liberty without "due process of law," as required by the 14th Amendment.[10]

Writing for the majority, Justice Hugo Black stated: "The First Amendment, as made applicable to the states by the 14th ... commands that a state 'shall make no law respecting an establishment of religion.'" Quoting Thomas Jefferson, Black noted that the First Amendment "erected a wall of separation between church and state." He concluded that "Neither a state nor the federal government can set up a church. Neither can pass laws which aid one religion, aid all religions, or prefer one religion over another."

Black's opinion was a turning point for the court. "This was the first instance in which the court interpreted the establishment clause as a restriction on the states," wrote James McClellan, chief counsel and staff director of the Separation of Powers Subcommittee of the Senate Judiciary Committee.[11] "It was a bold and revolutionary step, overturning more than a century and a half of established precedent that had uniformly permitted the states to set public policy regarding their relations with religious organizations." With the *Everson* decision, Black laid the foundation for the Supreme Court's rulings banning prayer and Bible readings in public schools.

Official Churches in American Colonies

History is replete with examples of wars and persecution over religion, the Crusades and the Spanish Inquisition being among

---

[10] The "Due Process Clause" reads: ". . . nor shall any State deprive any person of life, liberty or property, without due process of law. . . ."

[11] James McClellan, "The Making and the Unmaking of the Establishment Clause," in Patrick B. McGuigan and Randall R. Rader, eds., *A Blueprint for Judicial Reform*, Free Congress Research and Education Foundation (1981), p. 296.

the most notable. A little more than a century before the first settlement at Jamestown, Europe's historic domination by the Catholic Church had been shattered by the Protestant Reformation. Nations became internally divided over religious allegiances. Civil wars broke out over government attempts to suppress religious minority groups. Protestant sects even fought among themselves. It was in this context of intolerance that dissident religious minorities fled to find freedom in America. Yet, historians note that the settlers were quick to re-establish official churches. At the outbreak of the Revolution in 1775, nine of the 13 colonies had official churches.[12] By the time of the Constitutional Convention in Philadelphia in 1787, five retained official churches: Georgia, South Carolina, Connecticut, Massachusetts and New Hampshire.

Of the remaining eight colonies, only Virginia and Rhode Island shed all state ties with established religion. In their state constitutions, the others favored Protestants over Catholics, Jews, other minorities and non-believers. For example, New York officially discriminated against Catholics, New Jersey limited eligibility to public office to Protestants, and North Carolina required officeholders to declare belief in the Protestant religion and the divine inspiration of the Old and New Testaments. "On the eve of the Philadelphia Convention of 1787, the wall of separation doctrine espoused by Madison and Jefferson had been rejected in every state but Virginia and Rhode Island."[13]

The states, nonetheless, were reluctant to enter into a republic without a bill of rights guaranteeing certain fundamental freedoms, including freedom of religion. The Constitutional Convention had not adopted such guarantees because some participants feared that since all the desired freedoms could not be specified, any omitted from the document might possibly cease to be freedoms. Several of the states, however, ratified the Constitution with the understanding that the first order of business of the First Congress would be a bill of rights. Ten of the 12 proposed amendments were ratified and became part of the Constitution on Dec. 15, 1791.

Madison's and Jefferson's Views on Issue

The question, then, is what did the authors of the Constitution mean by the establishment clause of the First Amendment? Since the 1947 *Everson* case, the Supreme Court has espoused

---

[12] The Anglican Church in Virginia, New York, Maryland, South Carolina, North Carolina and Georgia, and the Congregational Church in Massachusetts, Connecticut and New Hampshire. From Robert L. Cord, *Separation of Church and State* (1982), p. 4.

[13] McClellan, *op. cit.*, pp. 300-306. Massachusetts was the last state to disestablish its official church, in 1833 — 44 years after ratification of the Constitution.

one answer, its critics another. The dispute centers on the writings and public actions of Thomas Jefferson and James Madison, who were the leading proponents of religious freedom among the framers of the Constitution. Justice Black summarized what has become the court's view of the historical record in the text of his *Everson* opinion. Black noted that Jefferson and Madison led the fight against Virginia's tax levy for support of the Anglican Church. It was during the legislative battle over the issue in 1785 that Madison wrote his famous "Memorial and Remonstrance Against Religious Assessments," in which he argued the state had no business taxing its citizens for support of religion. His arguments not only doomed the church tax but prepared the assembly to pass a year later the Virginia Statute for Religious Freedom, drafted by Jefferson.[14] The bill was a model of church-state separation. Later, as a member of the First Congress, Madison was chief architect of the First Amendment.

Jefferson, meanwhile, kept up with the Bill of Rights debate from his post in Paris as American minister to France. He coined the often cited term "separation of church and state" in an 1802 letter to the Danbury, Conn., Baptist Assembly. In it, he defended his record on religious liberty. While the phrase appears nowhere in the Constitution or the First Amendment, it was used by Black, and subsequently by other federal judges, to summarize the intent of the First Amendment's establishment clause.

On the strength of this record, the Supreme Court has ruled against state and local government involvement in public school religious exercises for two decades. But the court's interpretation of the record is flawed by omission and distortion, according to such critics as Robert Cord, professor of political science at Northeastern University in Boston. Cord, in his recent book *Separation of Church and State*, points out that Black omitted evidence that suggests Jefferson and Madison were not as absolute on the subject of church-state separation as the Supreme Court would have us believe.

For example, Jefferson in 1803 asked Congress to ratify a treaty with the Kaskaskia Indians that provided money to support a Catholic priest and build a church. As president, he did not veto three congressional extensions of a treaty entitled "An Act Regulating the Grants of Land Appropriated for Military Services and for the Society of the United Brethren for Propagating the Gospel Among the Heathen." The act used

---

[14] Jefferson biographer Dumas Malone has written that "Jefferson himself thought that his authorship of the Declaration of Independence and the Virginia Statute for Religious Freedom more deserving of remembrance than his presidency of the United States." See Dumas Malone, *Jefferson the Virginian* (1948), p. xii.

land grants to "purchase" the services of a religious order to settle Western lands for the benefit of Christian Indians. "Certainly Jefferson . . . would have vetoed these acts if he had believed that they violated the First Amendment," said Cord.[15]

Madison breached the wall of separation more often, according to Cord. Madison's "Memorial and Remonstrance Against Religious Assessments" frequently is cited as evidence that he was opposed to all state aid to religion. However, Cord notes that as a member of the Virginia General Assembly, Madison introduced a bill in 1785 entitled "A Bill for Punishing Disturbers of Religious Worship and Sabbath Breakers." It passed.

During the First Congress, Madison was a member of the House committee that recommended hiring a chaplain, a practice recently declared constitutional by the Supreme Court.[16] One day after the House voted to accept the First Amendment for ratification by the states, it passed a resolution asking President Washington to declare a national day of thanksgiving to praise God "for the many blessings he had poured down upon" the nation. Madison did not vote against the resolution. And although his papers after leaving the White House state his opposition to the practice, Madison, as president, declared four national days of thanksgiving between 1812 and 1815.

"In sum," says Cord, "as to the various interpretations that the U.S. Supreme Court — and the lower courts that have followed its decisions — have given to the Establishment Clause since the precedent case of *Everson* in 1947, I must conclude that the court has never logically, carefully, or fully considered all the available historical evidence and consequently has, for the most part, erred in its definition and application of the American constitutional doctrine of separation of Church and State." [17]

Evolution of the Supreme Court's Position

Following a different line of reasoning, other Supreme Court critics contend that the First Amendment was never intended to apply to the states, and that the court has improperly used the 14th Amendment to justify doing so. They cite judicial precedent. Speaking for a unanimous court in 1833, Chief Justice John Marshall wrote in *Barron v. Baltimore* that the first eight amendments "contain no expression indicating an intention to apply them to the state governments." In 1845, in

---

[15] Cord, *op. cit.*, p. 45.
[16] *Marsh v. Chambers*, decided July 5 by a 6-3 margin, upheld the Nebraska Legislature's practice of opening each session with a prayer by a chaplain paid by the state. The U.S. House and Senate have employed chaplains since 1789.
[17] Cord, *op. cit.*, p. 225.

"Released Time" Decisions:

McCollum v. Board of Education, 333 U.S. 203 (1948). The Champaign, Ill., school board operated a "released time" program in which religion teachers came into the public schools once a week to give 30 minutes of religious instruction to voluntary participants. By an 8-1 margin, the Supreme Court ruled the practice unconstitutional. "This is beyond all question a utilization of the tax-established and tax-supported public school system to aid religious groups to spread their faith," wrote Justice Hugo L. Black for the majority.

Zorach v. Clausen, 343 U.S. 306 (1952). The Supreme Court upheld, by a 6-3 vote, New York City's released time program, in which students were permitted to leave school buildings during the school day in order to receive religious instruction. The court found that "the public schools do no more than accommodate their schedules to a program of outside religious instruction."

Aid to Parochial Schools:

Everson v. Board of Education, 330 U.S. 1 (1947). The case involved a New Jersey statute that allowed local school boards to reimburse parents, including those whose children attended parochial school, for the costs of sending their children to school on public transportation. The Supreme Court, on a 5-4 vote, upheld the statute on the ground that it did not aid religion but was instead public welfare legislation benefiting children rather than schools. Historically more significant, however, was the court's observation that the "establishment of religion" clause of the First Amendment applied not just to the federal government, but to the states as well *(see p. 132)*.

Board of Education of Central School District No. 1 v. Allen, 392 U.S. 236 (1968). New York required local school boards to lend textbooks purchased with public funds to high school students, including those attending parochial schools. By a 6-3 vote, the Supreme Court upheld the law, saying its purpose was secular and neither advanced nor inhibited religion — the court's two tests for permissible state aid at that time *(see p. 139)*.

Lemon v. Kurtzman, 403 U.S. 602 (1971). Rhode Island authorized a salary supplement to certain non-public school teachers, but stipulated that recipient teachers must teach only secular subjects. By unanimous vote, the Supreme Court struck down the law and added a third test for permissible state aid: It must not foster excessive government entanglement with religion.

Prayer and Bible Readings:

Engel v. Vitale, 370 U.S. 421 (1962). The New York State Board of Regents recommended to school districts that they adopt a specified non-denominational prayer to be repeated voluntarily by students at the beginning of the school day. The New Hyde Park school board adopted the prayer and was sued by 10 students and the American Civil Liberties Union. State courts upheld the prayer on the basis that no student was compelled to participate. The Supreme Court ruled 6-1 against the state. Justice Black in the majority opinion stated: "[T]he constitutional prohibition against laws respecting an establishment of religion must at least mean that in this country it is no part of the business of government to compose official prayers for any group of the American people to recite as a part of a religious program carried on by the government."

School District of Abington Township v. Schempp and **Murray v. Curlett,** 374 U.S. 203 (1963). The *Abington* case concerned a Pennsylvania statute that required the reading of at least 10 verses of the Bible each day, followed by recitation of the Lord's Prayer. Students could be excused upon written request of the parents. The *Murray* case challenged a Baltimore city school board policy with similar requirements. The court ruled 8-1 that Bible readings in public schools were unconstitutional, and reaffirmed its position on recitation of prayers in public schools.

Voluntary School Prayer:

Karen B. v. Treen, 653 F. 2nd 897 (5th Cir. 1981). The Louisiana Legislature enacted a statute in 1980 that authorized school boards to permit students or teachers to offer a prayer at the beginning of the day. The U.S. District Court in the Eastern District of Louisiana ruled that voluntary prayer was constitutional. The 5th Circuit Court of Appeals reversed the lower court and ruled 2-1 that the statute was unconstitutional. The Supreme Court affirmed the Fifth Circuit ruling without comment in January 1982. This was the first time the high court had ruled in a case of prayer in the schools when no particular prayer had been prescribed by a governmental body.

Religious Observances:

Florey v. Sioux Falls School District 49-5, 619 F. 2nd 1311 (8th Cir. 1980), *cert. denied,* 449 U.S. 987 (1980). The Supreme Court refused to hear the case involving a school board policy that allowed singing of Christmas carols, performance of religious plays and the display of religious symbols in the Sioux Falls public schools. The U.S. District Court for the Southern District of South Dakota and the 8th District Court of Appeals declared the school board's policy constitutional.

Stone v. Graham, 449 U.S. 39 (1980). The Supreme Court struck down an 1978 Kentucky statute requiring that a permanent copy of the Ten Commandments be displayed in every classroom.

Permoli v. New Orleans, the court ruled that "the Constitution makes no provision for protecting the citizens of the respective states in their religious liberties; this is left to the state constitutions and laws."

Unlike the Bill of Rights, the 14th Amendment, ratified in July 1868, specifically included states in extending federal protection of life, liberty and property. For more than 50 years after its ratification, the court followed *Barron* and resisted pressure to construe the amendment to apply the Bill of Rights to the states. As late as 1922, the Supreme Court ruled in *Prudential Insurance Co. v. Cheek* that "neither the 14th Amendment nor any other provision of the Constitution imposes restrictions upon the states about freedom of speech [also protected by the First Amendment]." Two years later, however, the court reversed itself in *Gitlow v. New York* by declaring "for the present purposes we may and do assume that freedom of speech and of press which are protected by the First Amendment from abridgement by Congress — are among the fundamental personal rights and liberties protected by the due process clause of the 14th Amendment from impairment by the states." Thus began the gradual extension of the Bill of Rights to state and local governments through what became known as the Doctrine of Selective Incorporation.

A lot of critics of this extension argue that architects of the 14th Amendment never meant for it to apply the Bill of Rights to state and local governments. Why else, they ask, would House Speaker James G. Blaine, R-Maine, have introduced in 1875 a proposed constitutional amendment that provided: "No State shall make any law respecting an establishment of religion or prohibiting the free exercise thereof." Although the amendment failed, the fact that it was introduced indicates "there was a general understanding among the participants that the 14th Amendment left undisturbed the system of church-state relations established under the Bill of Rights," James McClellan wrote.[18]

At the time the Supreme Court struck down state-supported prayer and Bible reading in the early 1960s, an estimated 41 percent of the country's school districts permitted Bible reading and about half had some sort of devotional exercise.[19] The public outcry over the court's decisions resulted in open defiance and contempt. Billboards proclaimed "Impeach Earl Warren," the chief justice who led a judicially activist court in a series of controversial rulings on social issues. Twenty years after the prayer rulings, however, compliance is widespread.

---

[18] McClellan, *op. cit.,* p. 318.
[19] From by Lynn R. Buzzard, *Schools: They Haven't Got A Prayer* (1982), p. 52.

Six new appointees to the Court since Warren's retirement in 1969 have not brought about a new interpretation of church-state cases. In fact, it was Chief Justice Warren Burger who broadened the court's criteria for declaring state laws affecting religion unconstitutional. For 20 years the court had used two "tests" to make such a determination: Did the statute have a religious rather than secular purpose and did it either advance or inhibit religion? In *Lemon v. Kurtzman*, 1971 *(see box, p. 136)*, Burger added a third test: Did the law foster excessive government entanglement? Burger wrote the majority opinion that struck down a Rhode Island law allowing state salary supplements for parochial school teachers. The supplements resulted in excessive state entanglement with religion, the court found. Since then, the court has used the three-pronged test to overturn a Kentucky law requiring posting of the Ten Commandments in the classroom (*Stone v. Graham*, 1980), affirm a lower court ruling against a Louisiana law allowing voluntary school prayer (*Karen B. v. Treen*, 1982), and refuse to review a case in which lower courts permitted a school district to have Christmas observances (*Florey v. Sioux Falls School District*, 1980).

It is against this background of decisions that President Reagan and his supporters are pushing for a school prayer amendment. "It seems to the administration that it is desirable to return our society to the legal posture we had prior to 1962, and to state very clearly in the Constitution that voluntary prayer in the public schools is something that we should not discourage," Edward C. Schmults, deputy U.S. attorney general, told the Senate Judiciary Committee last year. Defenders of the high court contend that pleas for a return to a bygone era beg the real question. "The question that Congress must decide," Dean Terrance Sandalow of the University of Michigan Law School told the committee, ". . . is not a question of law, but a question of policy: whether the welfare of the nation would be served by removing from the Constitution all restrictions upon prayer in the public schools?" Five hundred professors of constitutional law and practicing attorneys said "no" in a petition Sandalow presented the committee.[20]

Religious Free Speech Issue

ATTEMPTS TO AMEND the Constitution to allow prayer and Bible reading in public schools are not new. No less

---

[20] Schumlts testified Aug. 18, 1982, and Sandalow on Sept. 16.

than 151 such amendments were introduced in 1964, the year after the Supreme Court struck down Bible reading in the *Abington* case.[21] None of those bills or subsequent ones succeeded. As the Senate prepares to vote once again on a school-prayer amendment, the old debate takes a new twist. If government-sponsored religious activity is what the courts forbid, then why can't students organize their own religious observances? This is the central question of the "religious free speech" or "equal access" issue. The Supreme Court has approved voluntary gatherings for college students, but so far it has banned them for public school students. The religious free speech issue has become a hot topic on Capitol Hill, where there is growing interest in bills proposed by Senators Denton and Hatfield to give student religious groups access to public schools. So far, Hatfield's bill has attracted the most support.

Interest in the religious free speech issue has grown steadily since the Supreme Court's *Widmar v. Vincent* decision on Dec. 8, 1981.[22] A University of Missouri student group called "Cornerstone" had requested access to campus facilities on the same basis as more than 100 other students groups. The University denied the request, citing its policy prohibiting religious meetings on campus. The Supreme Court ruled 8-1 against the university, holding that it could not deny use of its facilities for religious meetings if it allowed similar use by non-religious groups. The court also emphasized that "university students . . . are less impressionable than younger students and should be able to appreciate that the University's policy is one of neutrality towards religion."

Less than a week after the *Widmar* ruling, the court took a different stand on a case involving high school students in *Brandon v. Guilderland Central School District.*[23] It declined to review a circuit court of appeals decision involving a group of students at Guilderland High School in New York State who had asked the principal if they could meet for prayer in a classroom before the school day started. The principal and the school board said "no." The students brought suit, charging that the school board had violated their rights to free exercise of religion and speech. The 2nd Circuit Court of Appeals upheld a federal district court's denial of the students' request. The appeals court ruled:

> Our nation's elementary and secondary schools play a unique role in transmitting basic and fundamental values to our youth.

---

[21] See *1964 CQ Almanac*, p. 398.
[22] *Widmar v. Vincent*, 454 U.S. 263 (1981).
[23] *Brandon v. Board of Education of Gilderland Central School District*, 635 F. 2nd 971 (2nd Cir. 1980), *cert. denied*, 102 S. Ct. 970 (1981).

To an impressionable student, even the mere appearance of secular involvement in religious activities might indicate that the state has placed its imprimatur on a particular religious creed. This symbolic interference is too dangerous to permit.

In a similar case, the Supreme Court refused last January to review a lower court decision striking down the Lubbock, Texas, school board's policy allowing voluntary, student-initiated religious groups to meet in classrooms before or after school. The 5th Circuit Court of Appeals ruled in *Lubbock Civil Liberties Union v. Lubbock Independent School District* [24] that the seemingly neutral school policy had been adopted to circumvent the Supreme Court's school prayer decisions. "[T]he purpose of this policy, ostensibly devised to allow many groups to meet, is, when examined in the context of the total school policy, more clearly designed to allow the meetings of religious groups, " the appeals court said, adding that there was no evidence that non-religious groups had taken advantage of the policy.

Intent of Denton and Hatfield Measures

The *Lubbock* decision drew criticism from a broad spectrum of religious groups. And it gave fresh impetus for legislation on the religious free speech issue. Senators Denton and Hatfield introduced their bills within weeks after the *Lubbock* ruling. The Reagan administration has endorsed the intent of the bills. Secretary of Education T. H. Bell told the Senate Judiciary Committee in June, "The 'Equal Access' legislation . . . would merely put voluntary religious activity on an equal footing with other extracurricular activities permitted on public school premises."

The National Council of Churches, the National Association of Evangelicals and the Baptist Joint Committee support the Hatfield bill. Using the Supreme Court's logic in the *Widmar* case, the measure applies only to grades seven through 12 because secondary-level students are presumed old enough to distinguish between state neutrality and state support for religious exercises. Many religious groups oppose Denton's bill because it applies to grades kindergarten through 12. Elementary students are thought to be too young to understand that the schools must be neutral towards religion. Under both the Hatfield and Denton bills, school systems that did not allow students to meet at school facilities for religious purposes would have their federal funds cut off. The Hatfield bill stipulates that the meetings must be "voluntary and orderly," and it limits adult supervision to that necessary for security.

---

[24] *Lubbock Civil Liberties Union v. Lubbock Independent School District*, 669 F. 2nd 1038, (5th Cir. 1982), *cert denied*, 103 S. Ct. 800 (1983).

"Nothing in the Hatfield bill can be construed to allow state influence," said Forest Montgomery of the National Association of Evangelicals, who helped Hatfield's staff draft the bill. "With a whole bunch of caveats, the Hatfield bill says you can't forbid speech just because it is religious speech," said James Dunn, of the Baptist Joint Committee.

A spokesman for the American Civil Liberties Union argued that the Denton and Hatfield proposals were unnecessary "because the lower federal courts have been properly interpreting the Constitution, and Supreme Court precedent, in the cases that already have been decided." Jack D. Novik, an ACLU specialist in church-state affairs, said in a detailed memorandum that there were significant differences between the *Widmar* case and recent lower court decisions affecting public schools. The Supreme Court found in *Widmar* that the university had created an "open forum" by routinely permitting student groups to use empty classrooms for meetings. "Except for its prohibition against religious use, there was no record that the university had ever denied use of its facilities to a student group for content-related reason," Novik said.[25]

However, in *Brandon* and *Lubbock*, Novik argued, no "open forum" ever had been established by the schools. On the contrary, the Lubbock district had a decade-long history of resistance to Supreme Court prayer rulings. The student meeting policy declared unconstitutional was promulgated only after the Lubbock Civil Liberties Union filed suit to stop school-sponsored religious activities. Under the Lubbock meeting policy, "There was no evidence that any student groups other than religious groups had taken advantage of the policy, or that school facilities had actually been used as an open non-discriminatory public forum," said Novik. Facts in the *Brandon* case led Novik to a similar conclusion: "[T]here was no evidence that any other, non-religious student groups used the facilities or that the school had any policy permitting such use."

Novik concludes that the issue of religious free speech is best left to the courts. "The constitutionality of an extracurricular school-use policy depends upon the particular factual circumstances surrounding its adoption and implementation. Such sensitive and individualized judgments do not lend themselves to broad federal legislation," he wrote.

Continuing Controversy Over Prayer Issue

A federal district judge in Scranton, Pa., seemed to echo Novik's words of caution in a ruling on May 14, *Bender v.*

---

[25] Jack D. Novick, "The Constitutionality of Extracurricular Use of Public School Facilities for Religious Activities," American Civil Liberties Union, April 26, 1983.

Williamsport Area School District,[26] allowing students at the Williamsport High School to hold religious meetings during 30-minute free periods on Tuesday and Thursday mornings. Judge William J. Nealon said he relied on the Supreme Court's *Widmar* ruling to reach his decision, which he described as a "narrow one." "A slight change in the facts could very well have dictated a contrary decision," he said.

Following the *Widmar* precedent, Nealon held that the Williamsport High School had created a "limited forum" with a policy of permitting students to meet during activity periods. He noted that 25 other student groups had organized under the same policy. "The court is fully aware that the result reached in this case will not be free from doubt unless and until the Supreme Court clarifies two important areas of the law — the extent to which there can be a 'forum' for students in our high schools and the status of prayer in those institutions when initiated by the students acting independently of outside influences."

The *Bender* case, if upheld,[27] is likely to have repercussions far beyond the small central Pennsylvania city where it originated. Religious leaders cite school board opposition to the student group as an example of misinterpretation of the Supreme Court's ban on government-mandated prayer and Bible reading. The American Civil Liberties Union disagrees. John Shattuck, director of the ACLU Washington office, questioned the finding of even a "limited" open forum at Williamsport High. "Once you have an activity taking place during school hours, it is not a public forum because it is open only to students. I think the law and the courts have been very clear on this. A public school is not a public and open forum during school hours."

The ACLU's position on this and other church-state issues causes Cal Thomas of the Moral Majority to bristle with anger. ACLU lawyers, he said, have led a campaign to uproot the nation's religious traditions. Conservatives, he said, must learn that they, too, can fight for their beliefs in court, where "liberals" working for the ACLU have been so successful. Said Thomas: "We're organizing to go into court to take on these creeps on their own turf. The empire is about to strike back." It is clear that even if President Reagan's constitutional amendment and the Denton and Hatfield bills all are defeated, the school-prayer issue will not go away.

---

[26] *Bender v. Williamsport Area School District*, No. 82-0692 (M.D. Pa., May 12, 1983).
[27] The case has been appealed to the 3rd Circuit Court of Appeals.

Selected Bibliography

Books

Berns, Walter, *The First Amendment and the Future of American Democracy*, Basic Books, 1976.

Buzzard, Lynn R., *Schools: They Haven't Got A Prayer*, David C. Cook Publishing Co., 1982.

Cord, Robert L., *Separation of Church and State*, Lambeth Press, 1982.

Corwin, S. Edward, and J. W. Peltason, *Understanding the Constitution*, Holt, Rinehart and Winston, 1967.

Congressional Quarterly's Guide to the U.S. Supreme Court, Congressional Quarterly Inc., 1979.

McGuigan, Patrick B., and Randall R. Rader, eds., *A Blueprint for Judicial Reform*, Free Congress Research and Education Foundation, 1981.

Synder, Jill Donnie, and Eric K. Goodman, *Friend of the Court, 1947-1982*, Anti-Defamation League of B'nai B'rith, 1983.

Articles

Church and State (monthly publication of Americans United for Separation of Church and State, Silver Spring, Md.), selected issues.

Nixon, Robert W., "The Prayer Amendment: Another Round,"*Liberty*, March/April 1983.

Montgomery, Forest, "Another Class Distinction," *Action* (published by National Association of Evangelicals), May/June 1983.

Reports and Studies

Malbin, Michael J., "Religion and Politics, The Intentions of the Authors of the First Amendment," American Enterprise Institute, 1981.

Novik, Jack D., "The Constitutionality of Extracurricular Use of Public School Facilities for Religious Activities," American Civil Liberties Union, April 26, 1983.

Senate Judiciary Committee, "Proposed Constitutional Amendment to Permit Voluntary Prayer," July 29, Aug. 18 and Sept. 16, 1982, Government Printing Office, Serial No. J-97-129.

The MacNei'.-Lehrer Report, "School Prayer," May 6, 1982, Transcript #1724; "School Prayer," Sept. 22, 1982, Transcript #1823; Box 345, New York, N.Y. 10101.

Graphics: Cover illustration by George Rebh; cartoon p. 129 by Wayne Stayskal.

PRESSURES ON YOUTH

by

**Robert Benenson
and Sandra Stencel**

**Aug. 13
1 9 8 2**

PRESSURES ON YOUTH

I T USED to be said that children were meant to be seen, not heard. That is hardly the case today. During the past year, the problems of America's children and teen-agers captured headlines in newspapers and magazines across the country. One news magazine ran cover stories on "troubled teen-agers" and "neglected kids." [1] *The Washington Post* printed a seven-part series on "Coming of Age in the 80s." [2] *The New York Times* ran a six-part series on juvenile crime. [3]

Discussion of youth problems is not exactly uncharted territory. In 1904, G. Stanley Hall wrote a two-volume work entitled *Adolescence: Its Psychology and Its Relations to Physiology, Anthropology, Sex, Crime, Religion and Education.* Hall described adolescence as the "best key to the nature of crime. It is essentially antisocial, selfishness, refusing to submit to the laws of altruism." Popular culture, even in supposedly more innocent times, often dealt with troubled youths. Films such as "Angels with Dirty Faces" and "Public Enemy" in the 1930s, "Boys' Town" in the 1940s, and "The Blackboard Jungle," "Rebel Without a Cause" and "West Side Story" in the 1950s and early 1960s are just a few examples.

While adolescence has always been considered a difficult period, today's teen-agers seem more troubled than those of previous generations. Concern is increasing as the percentage of young Americans involved in aberrant or illicit behavior grows. Statistics on drug and alcohol abuse, sexual activity, juvenile crime and suicide are way up. Not only are more youths doing these things, they are doing them earlier.

"Coming of age in America is inescapably stressful," said Dr. Herbert Pardes, director of the National Institute of Mental Health. "For even the sturdiest of adolescents and their parents, the passage from childhood to adulthood is rarely smooth; for those already on unsteady ground, the transition can become turbulent and painful." [4]

---

[1] Stanley N. Wellborn, "Troubled Teen-agers," *U.S. News & World Report*, Dec. 14, 1981, pp. 40-47, and Alvin P. Sanoff and Jeanne Thornton, "Our Neglected Kids," *U.S. News & World Report*, Aug. 9, 1982, pp. 54-58.
[2] *The Washington Post*, Dec. 27, 1981-Jan. 2, 1982.
[3] *The New York Times*, Feb. 28-March 5, 1982.
[4] Foreword to "Adolescence and Stress: Report of an NIMH Conference," National Institute of Mental Health, 1981, p. iii.

Drug Use Among Students*

	Class of 1976	Class of 1977	Class of 1978	Class of 1979	Class of 1980	Class of 1981
Alcohol	85.7%	87.0%	87.7%	88.1%	87.9%	87.0%
Marijuana	44.5	47.6	50.2	50.8	48.8	46.1
Stimulants	15.8	16.3	17.1	18.3	20.8	26.0
Cocaine	6.0	7.2	9.0	12.0	12.3	12.4
Methaqua-lone	4.7	5.2	4.9	5.9	7.2	7.6
Heroin	0.8	0.8	0.8	0.5	0.5	0.5

*Percent who used in last 12 months.
Source: National Institute on Drug Abuse.

According to a poll of 160,000 teen-agers conducted by Jane Norman and Myron Harris for their book *The Private Life of the American Teen-ager* (1982), almost 60 percent of those aged 16-18 and 33 percent of those aged 13-15 have had sexual intercourse. Increased sexual activity among young people has meant an increase in the number of illegitimate births. In 1979, the latest year for which complete statistics are available, 33 percent of babies born to white teen-agers and 83 percent of those born to black teen-agers were illegitimate. More than half a million children live with unmarried teen-age mothers.[5]

Drug use among youths soared during the 1970s and remains high. Alcohol is the drug students try most often and are most likely to continue to use. According to the Department of Health and Human Services, about 15 percent of the nation's 10th to 12th graders are problem drinkers or at substantial risk for developing a drinking problem. More than seven million young persons between the ages of 12 and 17 — 31 percent of that age group — report having tried marijuana more than once. Among high school seniors, over 60 percent have experimented with marijuana. While marijuana use appears to have leveled off, use of other drugs continues to climb *(see box, above).*[6]

According to the Senate Subcommittee on Juvenile Justice, as many as one million children a year escape from their problems by running away from home. Many of these youngsters are victims of child abuse or neglect. They are also vulnerable to exploitation by pimps and pornographers. The National Committee for the Prevention of Child Abuse estimates that there may be as many as 600,000 child prostitutes in the nation.

Some desperate youths opt for the ultimate escape — suicide. Each year between 1,500 and 2,000 youths under age 20 are

[5] See "Sex Education," *E.R.R.*, 1981 Vol. II, pp. 633-652, and "Teen-age Pregnancy," *E.R.R.*, 1979 Vol. I, pp. 205-224.
[6] See "Marijuana Update," *E.R.R.*, 1982 Vol. I, pp. 105-124, and "Teen-age Drinking," *E.R.R.*, 1981 Vol. I, pp. 349-368.

listed as suicide victims.[7] While some youths take their frustrations out on themselves, many strike out at others. Young people traditionally have been responsible for a high percentage of crimes, but statistics indicate that youth crime is becoming more violent. According to the National Center for Juvenile Justice, juvenile arrests for violent crimes increased 41 percent from 1970 to 1979. The FBI reported that 1,237 persons under age 18 were arrested for murder in 1980.

Changing Environment and Expectations

Today's youth — defined as those under age 21 — were born after the post-World War II baby boom.[8] By past standards, they are a spoiled generation. They have grown up during a period when many people are affluent, most are comfortable and even the poor are cushioned against the severest devastations of poverty. They are the first generation for whom television, radio, the telephone, the automobile, even indoor plumbing, are virtually universal. On average, they have more leisure time, more money and more entertainment outlets, including today's omnipresent video games, than any previous generation.

But today's young people also were born and raised during a time of great political and social turmoil. Children as old as 18 were born after the assassination of President Kennedy. The Vietnam War, the 1960s youth revolt, the rising drug culture, soaring crime rates, inner-city riots, the civil rights movement, the women's liberation movement, Watergate, oil crises, the high-tech revolution, the arms race, television, runaway inflation and recession have all shaped the youth experience. So have the lifestyle changes of the past 20 years: rapidly rising divorce rates, single parenthood, two-income families, "the sexual revolution," overt homosexuality.

"Today's child has become the unwilling, unintended victim of overwhelming stress — the stress born of rapid, bewildering social change and constantly rising expectations," wrote child psychologist David Elkind. Adding to this stress, Elkind maintains, is the fact that society is forcing children to grow up too fast, to achieve too much in school and in sports, and to accept adult responsibilities before they are ready. "Children need time to grow, to learn, and to develop," he wrote in *The Hurried Child: Growing Up Too Fast Too Soon* (1981). "To treat them differently from adults is not to discriminate against them but rather to recognize their special estate."

---

[7] See "Youth Suicide," *E.R.R.*, 1981 Vol. I, pp. 429-448.

[8] The years most often given for the baby boom are 1946-61. In 1962, the U.S. fertility rate made its first sharp decline. However, the actual number of births remained high until 1965.

Some psychologists have criticized parents for using their children as tools in the battle to keep up with "the Joneses." In some ultra-competitive families children are judged not on the basis of their self-worth, but on their grades, clothes, extra-curricular activities, college acceptances and career goals. While some youngsters thrive on the pressure, others are not up to it. "The abysmal experience of being average with super-smart parents puts enormous pressures on a teen-ager," said Dr. C. Gibson Dunn of the Springwood Psychiatric Center in Leesburg, Va. "The goals his parents set for him are often so far away that anything he can do will never measure up." [9]

Analysts also accuse some parents of having warped priorities. "The parents are saying, 'I really think it is important for you to achieve, and when you do I'll think about loving you,'" said Harvard University psychologist Tom Cottle. "It is contingency love. Love on the bonus plan. It should be love no matter what." [10]

Growing Importance of Peer Relations

Not only are parents expecting more from their children, so are other children. "There is a dictatorship of peers," one 15-year-old student told a reporter. "You have to have a tan, clothes, good grades." [11] Some psychologists believe that because of the increase in divorce and the growth of two-income families *(see p. 155)*, peer groups are exercising more influence on children. "Many adolescents are no longer nested in an intact family, so the stresses on them are bound to be greater," said Dr. T. Berry Brazelton, an associate professor of pediatrics at Harvard Medical School. "They are more at the mercy of peer pressure than they were 20 years ago." [12]

Others attribute the growing importance of peer relations to parents' changing attitudes toward child-rearing. Many adults have come to believe that they are entitled to pursue their own interests — even if it means devoting less time to their children and making fewer sacrifices for them. "Parents are caught in a crunch of conflicting values," said Edward Weaver, director of the American Public Welfare Association. "They value children, but they value other things as well, such as time for themselves, material goods, status and their careers. Given these conflicts, in a number of instances they neglect their children or don't give them a fair shake." [13]

---

[9] Quoted in *The Washington Post*, July 4, 1981.
[10] Quoted by Wellborn, *op. cit.*, p. 43.
[11] Quoted in *The Washington Post*, July 4, 1981.
[12] Quoted in "The Secret to Raising Healthy, Happy Children," *U.S. News & World Report*, Dec. 14, 1981, p. 46. Brazelton is also chief of the child-development division at Children's Hospital Medical Center in Boston.
[13] Quoted by Sanoff and Thornton, *op. cit.*, p. 54.

Anorexia Nervosa

A growing number of teen-agers are responding to the pressures and stresses of modern life by resorting to self-destructive behavior. One example is a psychological disorder known as anorexia nervosa, often called "the starvation disease" because its victims starve themselves to the point of serious illness or death. The National Association of Anorexia Nervosa and Associated Diseases (ANAD), based in Highland Park, Ill., estimates that there are at least 500,000 victims of anorexia nervosa in the United States. There may actually be many more, said a spokeswoman for the organization, because anorexia is still a "closet disease," like alcoholism used to be.

Approximately 90 percent of the victims are female, although ANAD reports a growing number of males seeking treatment. Although most of the literature on the subject has dealt with well-to-do, adolescent girls, ANAD sees the "white, teen-age, upper-middle-class anorexic" as something of a stereotype — anorexics have been found as old as 85 and as young as eight, and ANAD studies have found no socioeconomic correlation to the disease.

Anorexics are controlled by a compulsive desire or need to lose weight. Most begin with modest dieting goals, but once started, they lose control and either refuse to or find they cannot stop. Many stop eating altogether or subsist on a few hundred calories per day. Some take laxatives or diuretics. Others — perhaps as many as 50 percent according to ANAD — become bulimic, which means they purposely regurgitate anything they have eaten before it is absorbed.

The symptoms of advanced anorexia can be devastating. Many anorexics deteriorate to weights as low as 60-65 pounds. In the most severe cases, the body starts to feed on its own proteins, essentially eroding itself. Vital organs may collapse from lack of sufficient nutrients. Between 10-15 percent of anorexia nervosa victims die, most commonly from heart and kidney failure.

There are differing theories about the causes of anorexia nervosa. Some experts attribute the problem to our society's emphasis on beauty and thinness. Psychologists also report that many of their young female victims are afraid of growing up and having to become independent, and attempt to forestall womanhood, which they effectively do since the disease usually results in the cessation of menstruation and breast development. Other psychologists say that anorexia is a result of repressed anger at parents or a desperate need for attention.

Like other compulsions and addictions, anorexia nervosa is extremely difficult to treat. A big problem is that many anorexics deny there is anything wrong with them. It is not unusual for a near-skeletal anorexic to claim that she or he is getting fatter.

Some experts believe too much emphasis is placed on the negative aspects of peer group relations. "Young adults and adolescents will always be subject to peer pressure," Dr.

Judianne Densen-Gerber said in a recent interview. "You do that so you can form your own family and your own attachments."[14] According to Dr. John Hill of the Boys Town Center for the Study of Youth Development, "slavish peer conformity" occurs primarily "when children are driven out of the family through some form of permissive neglect or extreme authoritarianism." [15]

New Concerns About Media's Influence

By the time the average child has graduated from high school, he or she will have spent 12,000 hours in the classroom and 18,000 hours watching television. The impact of television on children is a subject of much debate. Network executives insist there are no definitive studies indicating that television can be damaging to children. But the overwhelming majority of people responding to a recent poll (71 percent) agreed that violence on television produces aggressive behavior in children.[16]

Others are concerned about the relative lack of quality in children's programming and youngsters' increasing access to sexually explicit programs, including "R" and "X" rated movies shown on cable and subscription TV. David Elkind believes television contributes to the "hurried-child" syndrome."

> Young children are seeing more on television than their grandparents ever saw in a lifetime [he wrote]. By homogenizing age groups and appealing to the eighteen-to-forty-nine-year-old audience, television ... treats even young children as grown-up, as part of the large "common" audience. Consequently, even young children seem quite sophisticated about the major issues of our time — drugs, violence, crime, divorce, single parenting, inflation and so on.... But much of this knowledge is largely verbal. Adults, however, are often taken in by this pseudosophistication and treat children as if they were as knowledgeable as they sound.[17]

Studies indicate that the average child watches more than 20,000 television commercials a year.[18] Many adults are worried about the impact that all this advertising is having on the minds and bodies of the nation's youngest consumers — and on the wallets of their parents. "Childhood at times seems to be nothing more than a succession of material wants and yearnings: to

---

[14] Densen-Gerber is the founder and head of Odyssey Institute in New York City. The institute was founded in 1966 as a drug rehabilitation center, but has since expanded its areas of interests to include various child welfare issues including child abuse, child pornography and prostitution and age of consent.

[15] Speaking at a conference on "Adolescence and Stress" sponsored by the National Institute of Mental Health in September 1980.

[16] Findings of "The Merit Report: A Public Opinion Survey" conducted June 8-13, 1982. "The Merit Report" is sponsored by Merit cigarettes.

[17] David Elkind, *The Hurried Child: Growing Up Too Fast Too Soon* (1981), p. 77.

[18] See E. Kaye, *The ACT Guide to Children's Television* (1979).

eat Big Macs, to play with Tonka trucks, to wear Underoos, to go camping with Barbie and Ken," Christopher Johnson wrote in *Today's Education.*[19]

Sexual overtones in recent ads for all sorts of kids' products, especially blue jeans, have prompted a rash of criticism. "What's disturbing about these commercials is that they open up a new frontier by portraying boys and girls in very sexual situations," said Kim Hays of Action for Children's Television (ACT). "We feel it's important for 12- and 13-year-olds to know about sex, but not the way advertisers present it." [20]

The most controversial jean ads feature teen-age actress and model Brooke Shields making what some regard as sexually enticing testimonials. "What comes between me and my Calvins (Calvin Klein jeans)?" Shields asked in one ad. "Nothing," came the reply. Viewers' complaints about her body language led the three major television networks to ban what one executive called "the more explicit commercials."

Many observers are concerned about the image of teen-age sexual precocity portrayed in such recent films as "Pretty Baby," "Endless Love," "Taxi Driver," "Foxes" and "The Blue Lagoon." Also objectionable to many child welfare advocates are rock music lyrics that, they say, glorify sex and drug use. "Permitting kids . . . to have as role models pop singers who sing about drugs is a disaster," said Dr. Densen-Gerber. Rep. Robert K. Dornan, R-Calif., recently introduced a bill in Congress that would require warning labels on record albums that he says contain hidden messages extolling satanic worship. A similar bill was introduced in the California Legislature.

Economic Pressures: Education and Jobs

Children were never entirely spared from economic troubles. Poverty has always severely affected the young. It was not until the early part of this century that child labor laws were passed to protect children from economic exploitatin *(see box, p. 157).* But today, economic pressures are not limited to poor youths, but are being felt by middle-class and upper middle-class youngsters who were long sheltered from economic uncertainties. Probably the greatest worry of youths from all economic backgrounds is that they will be the first generation to be less well off than their parents.

"America has been built on the idea of upward mobility,"

---

[19] Christopher Johnson, "The Standardized Child," *Today's Education,* November-December 1981, p. 27.

[20] ACT, a Boston-based group of parents and educators founded in 1968, is the leader of the movement to restrict advertising on children's television programs and is responsible for many of the reforms in children's programming.

Photo by Ken Heinen

Today's youth may be less well off than their parents.

wrote Robert J. Samuelson, "but the current slump — actually
the entire economic experience of the past decade — has raised
the specter of downward mobility. Seditious though it sounds,
it's an idea that is clearly troubling a lot of Americans." [21]
Nearly 70 percent of those responding to a March 8, 1982,
Washington Post-ABC News Survey thought they were better
off than their parents, but only 43 percent thought their children would be in the same position.

One reason for this kind of pessimism is that today's youths
were preceded into the job market by the 65 million members of
the "baby boom." This group, which includes the parents of
some of today's children, is the best educated and, despite the
nation's recent economic problems, the most upwardly mobile
generation in American history. And because of the size of the
baby boom group, the generation following it may find the paths
to success blocked by their elders. This problem may be partially offset by early training of young people in new, expanding
technologies. But when many of today's youths reach their 30s
and 40s, they may find the executive and managerial positions
they seek already occupied.

The nation's economic retrenchment, the highly competitive
job market, the decline of high-paying blue-collar jobs and the
transition to a computer-and-technology oriented society have
made a college education increasingly important. At the same
time, higher education is becoming more difficult to attain.
According to the National Center for Educational Statistics,
tuition costs at public colleges rose an average of 66 percent

[21] Robert J. Samuelson, "Downward Mobility," *National Journal,* July 31, 1982, p. 1347.

from 1974-75 to 1981-82; private college tuition went up 89 percent. College loans are harder to obtain and are available only at high interest rates. Federal student aid programs have been trimmed by the Reagan administratin *(see box, p. 160).* Unless these economic conditions change, many more young people will have to defer their college education, start working younger and longer to save for college, go to college part-time while holding part- or full-time jobs, or forgo college altogether.

For those youths who do not obtain a higher education, especially those from poorer households, the changing economy is creating new pressures. Unskilled blue-collar jobs, a traditional outlet of opportunity for poor youths, are disappearing as factories close or workers are replaced by machines.[22] Even the part-time jobs where young people have gotten a start, such as in fast-food restaurants and supermarkets, are being competed for by hard-pressed adults. Youth unemployment in July was 24.1 percent; black youth unemployment was 49.7 percent.

Changes in the Family

WHILE today's youth may face special problems, adolescence has long been recognized as a period of development fraught with stressful aspects. Adolescence "is a period of extraordinary change, multiple conflicts and marked societal demands upon the individual for the successful completion of significant developmental tasks," wrote Dr. Norman Garmezy of the University of Minnesota. "On the side of change, there are the hormonal, physiological and somatic changes that are reflected in pubertal development.... Equally important psychological changes are spurred on by this rapid physical development.... As for conflict, this tends to be focused on parents as the most significant adults in the life of the adolescent." [23]

Intensifying the usual parent-child conflicts have been the extraordinary changes in family life in the past two decades.[24] A report issued by the National Center for Health Statistics in November 1980 projected that one of every two marriages in the United States will eventually end in divorce.[25] In 1981, according to the Census Bureau, there were over 1.2 million divorces in the United States. About 5.5 million children under age 18 were living with a divorced parent last year.

---

[22] See "America's Employment Outlook," *E.R.R.*, 1982 Vol. I, pp. 385-408 and "The Robot Revolution," *E.R.R.*, 1982 Vol. I, pp. 345-364.
[23] Overview to "Adolescence and Stress: Report of an NIMH Conference," *op. cit.*, p. 3.
[24] See "Changing American Family," *E.R.R.*, 1977 Vol. I, pp. 413-432.
[25] The report, "National Estimate of Marriage Dissolution and Survivorship," was written by Dr. James A. Weed, who is now with the U.S. Census Bureau.

Divorce can have serious psychological consequences for children and adolescents. Even when custody is not contested, parents often confuse children by competing for their loyalties. Aside from the obvious disruption of the normal family routine, divorce frequently threatens a child's sense of security because of the family's diminished economic circumstances or the child's fear of losing the remaining parent. Some children blame themselves for their parents' problems.

Divorce often thrusts children into roles for which they are not prepared. For instance, some divorced parents turn to their children for friendship. "I debrief with the kids when I get home from work the way I used to with my husband...," said one divorced mother. "I guess I tell them more than I ought to about my worries, but they might as well find out sooner or later that life can be complicated, unfair and infuriating." [26] Psychologist David Elkind is among those who believe parents should not put such burdens on their children. "Children are hurried into mature interpersonal relations because the parent is under stress and needs a confidant...," he wrote. "Unfortunately ... it is by no means clear that this is what the child needs." [27]

The Implications of Women's Employment

One of the most significant changes in family lifestyles in recent years has been the increase in the number of working women. Over half of the adult female population is now in the labor force. According to the Bureau of Labor Statistics, over half of all children under age 18 have working mothers. [28] The Census Bureau reported July 29 that 45 percent of all mothers of preschool children were working in 1980, up fourfold from 1950.

The arrival of the two-paycheck family has been accompanied by a redefinition of family roles. As women contribute more to families' economic welfare, their husbands and children are expected to do more around the house. In many households, children are expected not only to do the dishes and clean their rooms, but to do the family grocery shopping, cook some of the meals and help care for younger children.

In the past the children of working mothers were usually cared for in the home by grandparents or other relatives. Today, however, 48.7 percent of the children of full-time working mothers are cared for in day-care centers or by babysitters who are not related to the child. For preschoolers, this figure is 62

---

[26] Quoted by Marie Winn in "What Became of Childhood Innocence?" *The New York Times Magazine*, Jan. 25, 1981, p. 16.

[27] Elkind, *op. cit.*, p. 42.

[28] Allyson Sherman Grossman, "More Than Half of All Children Have Working Mothers," *Monthly Labor Review*, February 1982, pp. 41-43.

Child Labor

The Reagan administration caused a flap July 16 when it announced proposed regulations concerning work rules for 14- and 15-year-olds. The regulations would broaden the hours and types of jobs that could be performed by children in this age group. Opposition from labor, parent, teacher and child protection groups resulted in the withdrawal of the proposed regulations pending further review.

Child labor has not been much of a national issue in recent years, but it certainly was one earlier in the century. Hundreds of thousands of children, many of them under age 10, performed dirty and often dangerous work in coal mines, glass factories, cigarette and textile mills and other industrial locations. A widespread movement evolved to protest child labor. Although a number of states passed child labor laws, similar efforts at the federal level were often thwarted. The Supreme Court ruled congressional child-labor laws unconstitutional in 1918 and 1922. In 1924, a constitutional amendment controlling child labor was passed by Congress, but was not ratified by enough states.

Finally, in 1938, Congress passed child labor regulations that stood up as part of the Fair Labor Standards Act. This law set 14 as the minimum age for non-manufacturing work outside of school hours, 16 for employment in interstate commerce during school hours, and 18 for hazardous occupations. Children aged 14 and 15 were not permitted to work after 7 p.m., were allowed to work only three days and 18 hours during the school week, and were barred from "dangerous" jobs such as operating and repairing power-driven kitchen implements, such as food slicers and grinders.

The changes that the Reagan administration is considering would affect these regulations. Children 14 and 15 would be allowed to work until 9 p.m. on school nights and until 10 p.m. on non-school nights. The work week would be expanded to four days and 24 hours, and the prohibition against certain types of work would be lifted. William Otter, the Department of Labor's wage and hour administrator, told the House Labor Standards Subcommittee July 28 that the new rules would "improve the employment opportunities of young workers without harming their health, well-being or opportunity for schooling." But Thomas Donahue, secretary-treasurer of the AFL-CIO, said that the regulations would "create a pool of cheap, part-time child labor, the beneficiaries of which would be the various industries that already have notorious records for violating and undercutting fair labor standards."

percent. Many parents find private day-care or babysitting arrangements unsatisfactory, unavailable or too expensive. Public day care is available only to a very small percentage of children. The result is that many children are left on their own all day or return to empty houses after school. There are an estimated 4-10 million of these so-called "latchkey" children.

For some youngsters, the "latchkey" experience provides valuable lessons in responsibility, caution and independence. But experts in child development say that being left alone for long periods can be harmful for many children. Professor Lynette Long of Loyola College in Baltimore said that almost all the latchkey children she interviewed for an upcoming book on the subject had frequent nightmares about someone breaking into their homes.[29] Police say latchkey children are particularly susceptible to attack or injury. The lack of adult company and guidance may also contribute to juvenile crime. For example, when a Portland, Ore., YMCA began a program for latchkey children, vandalism at three local schools fell from $12,000 to $200 in one year.

Severity of Child Abuse, Neglect Problem

Child abuse and neglect have always been around, but experts say the problem is on the rise. The American Humane Association (AHA) reported that there were 788,844 official reports of child maltreatment in 1980, involving an estimated 1.2 million children. This represented a 91 percent increase over 1976. Many other incidents were never reported.[30]

Some of the increase may be attributable to more accurate data-gathering efforts, but child abuse authorities say the increases are real. Dr. Ann H. Cohn, executive director of the National Committee for the Prevention of Child Abuse (NCPCA), told Editorial Research Reports that even in areas where advertising and public awareness about child abuse have been evident for a long time, child abuse statistics have shown a significant increase. "If you talk to protective service workers in every major city, there's been increasing numbers of really serious cases of child abuse, dramatic increases in the numbers of deaths due to child abuse," she said. According to the American Humane Association, 20 percent of child abuse victims suffer minor physical injury and 4 percent suffer major physical injury. NCPCA estimates that between 2,000 and 5,000 youngsters die each year as a result of child abuse.

Cohn believes there are two primary factors behind the recent increase in child abuse: (1) the nation's economic problems, which produce severe stress for many families and create the volatile atmosphere in which abuse can occur; and (2) the fact that many of the social, health and day-care services that were available to low-income families are being scaled back or eliminated by government budget cutting. "I think as we start to pull those supports away from families, we also will see increasing amounts of child abuse," Cohn said.

---

[29] Quoted by Stanley N. Wellborn in "When School Kids Come Home to an Empty House," *U.S. News & World Report*, Sept. 14, 1981, pp. 42-47.
[30] See "Violence in the Family," *E.R.R.*, 1979 Vol. I, pp. 305-324.

About 7 percent of reported child abuse victims, or approximately 84,000 youngsters, were sexually abused. "There seems little doubt that the incidence of sexual abuse committed against children is vastly higher than anyone would like to believe," stated an NCPCA pamphlet, "with the shocking possibility that the annual incidence could be in excess of 1,000,000." Cohn said that 90 percent of teen-age prostitutes claim to have been sexually abused as children.

Coping With the Problem

ALL THE attention given to youth problems in recent years has prompted a get-tough attitude among many adults. This is particularly true in the area of juvenile justice. "There is little doubt among juvenile justice experts — or legislators who specialize in the field — that a heightened public awareness of juvenile crime is creating pressures for a crackdown on what is seen as the softness and lenience of juvenile courts," Richard W. Foster wrote in a magazine published by the National Conference of State Legislatures in Denver, Colo.[31]

New York was one of the first states to enact special legislation to toughen treatment of juvenile offenders. A 1976 law required minimum sentences for youths judged to be responsible in juvenile courts for certain violent crimes. A 1978 law facilitated waivers of youthful offenders to adult courts for certain violent felonies. According to Foster, other states have followed the current trend in adult justice and set minimum or fixed sentences for juveniles convicted of crimes.

Parents themselves are sometimes resorting to tough measures to control unruly children. In 1980, professional youth counselors David and Phyllis York of Lansdale, Pa., founded the "Toughlove" movement, which advocates strict parental discipline. The Yorks developed this approach after their own daughter repeatedly got into trouble. The theory behind Toughlove is that forgiving or accepting the behavior of troublemaking children, no matter how well meaning, is often ineffective or counterproductive. "It's just old-time discipline, where parents run the home and there is cooperation among family members," said one member.[32]

---

[31] Richard W. Foster, "Juvenile Justice in the United States," *State Legislatures*, January 1982, p. 20.
[32] Quoted in *Time*, June 8, 1981.

Student Aid Reductions

When the Reagan administration came to office in 1981, federal aid to college students was one of those areas targeted for budget savings. Student aid had been one of the fastest growing federal programs. According to the Senate Budget Committee, federal spending on the guaranteed student loan (GSL) program grew by 82 percent between 1976 and 1981.

The major targets of White House and congressional budget cutters were the two largest student aid programs: the Pell grants (named after Sen. Claiborne Pell, D-R.I.), which in fiscal year 1981 provided 2.7 million mainly lower- and lower-middle-class students with an average of $838 in grants-in-aid, and the guaranteed student loan program, which provided interest subsidies to banks and guaranteed payments of loans to 3.5 million mainly middle-class students in fiscal year 1981. According to the Congressional Budget Office, cuts ordered in last year's budget reconciliation law will result in the reduction or elimination of guaranteed loans to families with incomes over $30,000. Pell Grants will be reduced by an average of $80. Approximately 650,000 students who had been receiving Social Security benefits as children of retired, disabled or deceased workers will have their benefits reduced by an average of $2,500 in 1983.

The 1983 budget proposal submitted by the president to Congress this year included further cuts in federal student aid. This time, though, the budget proposals were met with united and fierce opposition from education and student lobbies. On March 1, a National Student Lobby Day drew 5,000 students to Washington to demonstrate against the budget cuts and to lobby representatives and senators to vote against them.

The Senate Budget Committee reduced the proposed cuts, but Senate Republican leaders decided even this was too much, given the political pressure, and dropped the student aid cuts altogether. The Democratic-controlled House committees did likewise. When reconciliation instructions were sent to committees following the passage in June of the first budget resolution, no cuts were ordered in student aid programs.

A spokesman for Toughlove said there were about 600 chapters in 48 states, Canada, West Germany, Britain and Guam. Members act as a support group for other parents, sharing experiences and offering advice. Members are encouraged to set strict rules and to punish children if they misbehave or get into trouble. Less severe punishments might include removal of telephone and automobile privileges or curfews. If children continue to cause trouble within or outside the home, Toughlove parents may lock them out of the house, supplying them with the names of other members who have agreed to take them in until they agree to live by the family rules. If a problem becomes incorrigible, Toughlove encourages parents to instruct children to get professional help or move out. Toughlove also discourages parents from bailing their children out if they get into trouble with the police.

Some mental health experts have reservations about the Toughlove program. Dr. Lawrence A. Brain, a psychiatrist from Bethesda, Md., believes universal solutions can be dangerous when dealing with the individual, often delicate, psychological problems of a troubled youth. When dealing with children under age 18, he said, "structure must be set up in a flexible and compassionate way." [33] Many psychiatrists believe that except in extreme circumstances children should never be thrown out of the house. "The more disturbed the child is, the more cautious one should be about letting him go," said Dr. Toksoz B. Karasu, chairman of the American Psychiatric Association's Commission on Psychiatric Therapies.[34]

Attempts to Control Kids' Sexual Activity

Many adults, especially those who are politically conservative, are attempting to control children's sexual behavior. The Reagan administration is considering a regulation that would require federally funded family planning clinics to notify parents when children under age 18 are given birth control prescriptions. Supporters blame the easy availability of contraceptives for the rise in youth sexuality. Opponents say it will simply scare sexually active youths away from family planning clinics, resulting in more teen-age pregnancies.

Last year Congress authorized funding for a controversial teen-age sexuality program that its supporters hoped would help discourage sexual activity among teen-agers. The program, funded at $30 million a year for three years, continued an existing program that provided pregnant teen-agers with prenatal care and counseling. But it also provided funds for "preventive services," which were to be provided by maternity homes, YWCAs and others who operate programs for pregnant teen-agers. As originally drafted by Sen. Jeremiah Denton, R-Ala., the bill called for the promotion of teen-age "chastity" as a solution to "the problem of adolescent promiscuity," but that language was dropped.[35]

Teen-age sexuality was one of the issues discussed at a recent conference, Family Forum II, sponsored by the Moral Majority Foundation and other "New Right" groups. More than 500 adherents of the so-called "pro-family movement" attended the July 27-29 conference and heard such speakers as Dr. J. Craig Perry, special assistant on child and family issues to Sen. Orrin

[33] Quoted in *The Washington Times*, July 21, 1982.
[34] Quoted in *The New York Times*, May 14, 1982.
[35] See *1981 CQ Almanac*, pp. 487-488.

Teen-agers are more likely to make choices their
parents like when they are not pushed to do so.

G. Hatch, R-Utah, and George Gilder, author of *Wealth and
Poverty* (1980). Perry told the group that their tax dollars were
paying for such things as "sex education programs that are in
contradiction with the Bible" and "adolescent and family planning programs that say to children ... 'Your parents are old-
fashioned and so we will explain sex to you and help you avoid
having a baby.' "

A Different View of Adolescent Behavior

While some adults are concentrating on ways to control
adolescent behavior, Dr. Richard Jessor, a University of Colorado psychologist, has suggested that such things as cigarette
smoking, alcohol and drug use, sexual activity and physical
aggressions may be part of normal adolescent development and
play an important role in the process of transition to young
adulthood. "The argument can be made that coming to terms
with alcohol, drugs and sex has emerged as a new developmental
task that all adolescents face as part of the normal process of
growing up in contemporary American society," he said in a
paper presented at the 10th annual Schering Symposium on
Adolescence held during the annual American School Health
Association convention last fall.[36] "Since problem behavior is ...
unlikely to disappear," Jessor concluded, it is important to
understand it and attempt to reduce its negative personal and
social consequences.

[36] Excerpts from his remarks reprinted in *PTA Today*, May 1982, p. 23.

Pressures on Youth

According to psychologists Robert and Jean Bayard, parents have to recognize that they cannot dictate their children's behavior. "In their love and concern for their children, parents often decide how the children should behave, and then push them to do so — to do their homework, to choose the 'right' sort of friends, and so on," they wrote. "Well meant as this may be, it nonetheless tends to lower teen-agers' self-esteem and make them unsure of their abilities to make their own decisions." Instead, they suggest that parents put the responsibility for the teen-ager's decisions squarely on his or her own shoulders. "This is not easy for many parents," they said, "but it can have powerful positive effects in improving the family situation. Paradoxically, teen-agers seem *more* likely to make choices their parents like when they are not pushed to do so."[37]

It is worth noting that most children make the transition to adulthood with few permanent scars. As reporter Dan Morgan noted in *The Washington Post:* "Statistics show 90 percent of high school students do not use drugs frequently; 94 percent do not drink alcohol every day; 97 percent have not used a knife or gun to get something from somebody else; 97 percent have never struck a teacher, and 85 percent of teen-age girls never get pregnant." [38] Apparently, most children do know what is in their best interests.

---

[37] Robert T. Bayard and Jean Bayard, "How To Deal With Your Acting-Up Teen-ager," *PTA Today,* May 1982, p. 22.
[38] *The Washington Post,* Dec. 27, 1981.

Selected Bibliography

Books

Califano, Joseph A. Jr., *The 1982 Report on Drug Abuse and Alcoholism*, Warner, 1982.

Elkind, David, *The Hurried Child: Growing Up Too Fast Too Soon*, Addison-Wesley, 1981.

Keniston, Kenneth, *All Our Children: The American Family Under Pressure*, Harcourt Brace Jovanovich, 1977.

Offer, Daniel, Eric Ostrov and Kenneth I. Howard, *The Adolescent: A Psychological Self-Portrait*, Basic, 1981.

Articles

Cevoli, Cathy, "Is There Anything a 28-Year-Old Can Teach Her Teenage Sister (That She Doesn't Already Know)?" *Ms.,* February 1982.

Foster, Richard W., "Juvenile Justice in the States: Which Way Is It Heading?" *State Legislatures,* January 1982.

Grossman, Allyson Sherman, "More Than Half of All Children Have Working Mothers," *Monthly Labor Review,* February 1982.

Helgesen, Sally, "Theoretical Families," *Harper's,* January 1982.

Johnson, Christopher, "The Standardized Childhood," *Today's Education,* December 1981.

Long, Lynette and Thomas J. Long, "What To Do When The Children Are Home Alone," *Essence,* March 1982.

O'Roark, Mary Ann, "The Alarming Rise in Teenage Suicide," *McCall's,* January 1982.

Sanoff, Alvin P., et al., "Our Neglected Kids," *U.S. News & World Report,* Aug. 9, 1982.

Wellborn, Stanley N., "Troubled Teen-agers," *U.S. News & World Report,* Dec. 14, 1981.

___ "When Kids Come Home To An Empty House," *U.S. News & World Report,* Sept. 14, 1981.

Reports and Studies

Editorial Research Reports: "Marijuana Update," 1982 Vol. I, p. 107; "Youth Suicide," 1981 Vol. I, p. 431; "Teen-age Drinking," 1981 Vol. I, p. 351; "Juvenile Justice," 1979 Vol. II, p. 543; "Violence in the Family," 1979 Vol. I, p. 307; "Teen-age Pregnancy," 1979 Vol. I, p. 205.

National Center for Juvenile Justice, "The Serious Juvenile Offender: The Scope of the Problem and the Response of Juvenile Courts," September 1981.

National Committee for Prevention of Child Abuse, "An Approach to Child Abuse," 1981.

National Institute of Mental Health, "Adolescence & Stress: Report of a NIMH Conference," 1981.

National Institute on Alcohol Abuse and Alcoholism, "Alcohol Topics In Brief," 1980.

National Institute on Drug Abuse, "Highlights from Student Drug Use in America 1975-1981," 1982.

Cover illustration by Staff Artist Cheryl Rowe;
photos p. 154 and p. 162 by Ken Heinen.

CHANGING ENVIRONMENT IN COLLEGE SPORTS

by

Robert Benenson

Apr. 15
1 9 8 3

Editor's Note: After the signing of University of Georgia star running back Herschel Walker by the New Jersey Generals in February 1983, the United States Football League (USFL) announced its intention to observe the pro football rule barring the signing of undergraduate college players (or college dropouts who would be undergraduates if they remained in school).

However, on Feb. 29, 1984, U.S. District Judge Laughlin E. Waters held the USFL rule illegal, calling it a "group boycott" forbidden by the Sherman Antitrust Act. On March 3, the New Orleans Breakers of the USFL signed 19-year-old running back Marcus DuPree. DuPree had starred as a freshman at University of Oklahoma in 1982 but dropped out because of disagreements with the team coaching staff. He enrolled at University of Southern Mississippi in 1983 with the intention of playing there but dropped out in January 1984 when the National Collegiate Athletic Association, under its transfer rules, said he would be ineligible until the 1985 season.

The suit that resulted in the court ruling was brought by a player seeking entrance to the USFL and had no bearing on the similar rule observed by the National Football League. On March 19, NFL commissioner Pete Rozelle announced that the league would continue to observe the rule until forced by law to accept undergraduates.

CHANGING ENVIRONMENT
IN COLLEGE SPORTS

W HEN the National Football League (NFL) stages its annual draft of college players on April 26, much of the
attention will focus on those players who are not selected. NFL
officials have stated that the league intends to maintain its 48-
year-old prohibition against drafting players who have not completed their college eligibility.[1] Eligibility rules became the center of controversy last February when the NFL's new competi-
tor, the United States Football League (USFL),[2] broke tradition
by signing University of Georgia star running back Herschel
Walker after his junior year. Walker, 1982 winner of the
Heisman Trophy, an award given to the player voted the best in
college football, signed a three-year contract worth an estimated
$3.9 million with the USFL's New Jersey Generals.

Although the Herschel Walker incident was the most publicized issue involving college sports in recent months, it was by
no means the only one. Years of concern over educational standards, commercialism and professionalism, recruiting scandals,
and the movement for women's athletic equality have inspired
passage of new rules by the National Collegiate Athletic Association (NCAA) and intensified demands for change from various
quarters.

Much of the impetus for change has come from college administrators, many of whom previously tended to stay aloof from
controversies involving intercollegiate athletics. "College and
university presidents are taking a very active role," said Bob
Aaron, public affairs director for the American Council on
Education.[3] For instance, college presidents were in the forefront of the drive that recently led the NCAA to upgrade
academic eligibility requirements for student athletes.

[1] Under NCAA rules, athletes are eligible to participate in varsity sports for four years. If
an athlete should miss a year because of injury or another reason, he may complete his
eligibility in a fifth year as an enrolled student. The NFL enacted its rule against drafting
students with remaining eligibility in 1925 in reaction to the controversy that erupted when
the fledgling league signed running back Harold E. "Red" Grange, one of the great college
players of his time, after his junior year at the University of Illinois.
[2] Despite the negative reactions from some quarters, the signing of Walker was a publicity
boon for the USFL, which previously lacked a star attraction for its untried concept of
spring football. The 1983 USFL regular season runs from March 6 to July 3, with playoffs to
follow.
[3] The American Council on Education, located at 1 Dupont Circle, N.W., Washington,
D.C. 20036, conducts research and publishes reports on various educational subjects. Its
members include colleges, universities and education associations.

After Herschel Walker signed with the New Jersey Generals, several coaches vowed to bar USFL scouts from their campuses. The league declared its innocence in the affair, pointing out that Walker and his lawyer, Jack Manton, had approached them first, not the other way around.[4] Nevertheless, USFL Commissioner Chet Simmons announced that the prohibition on recruiting players with remaining eligibility would be reinstated and enforced. The NFL, which had loudly criticized the Walker signing, reaffirmed that it would abide by the rule during its 1983 player draft in April.

This did not end the controversy, however, since many players and their representatives have questioned the legality of the eligibility rule. A similar rule by the National Basketball Association (NBA) was found unconstitutional over a decade ago. Judge War-

Herschel Walker

ren J. Ferguson of the Federal District Court in Los Angeles ruled in 1971 that the NBA rule constituted an illegal "restraint of trade" that prevented basketball players from seeking employment in their desired occupation.[5] USFL officials, citing this decision, said the league decided to sign Walker rather than face a court challenge that could have wiped the rule completely off the books.[6]

Having used this explanation to rationalize the Walker signing, the USFL has placed itself in a difficult position. If, as league counsel Steven Ehrhart stated, "It is impossible under current law to ignore a young athlete's right to pursue employment and career opportunities just as any other individual enjoys the same right," [7] then the USFL might be accused of

---

[4] Under NCAA rules, Walker lost his college eligibility simply by negotiating with a professional team. Even if the USFL had not given Walker a contract, he would have been ineligible to play college football.

[5] After the 1971 court decision, the NBA passed what was known as the "hardship rule," which stated that college players with remaining eligibility had to prove financial need in order to leave school early to play for the pros. The hardship requirement was dropped in 1976, however, as a result of a collective bargaining agreement with the NBA players' union.

[6] The NFL bent its own rule in 1977 when it permitted Al Hunter, a junior running back at Notre Dame who had been declared ineligible for disciplinary reasons, to sign with its Seattle team. Hunter had threatened to sue if he was not permitted to play.

[7] Ehrhart made the comment on March 17, 1983, before a Senate Judiciary Committee hearing on "The Collegiate Student Athlete Protection Act of 1983" *(see p. 169)*.

restraint of trade the next time it resists the overtures of a player who wants to leave college early. But if the league signs other players with remaining eligibility, it will again be accused of "raiding" and threatened with sanctions by college coaches.

A bill has been introduced in the Senate that would legitimize the eligibility rule. "The Collegiate Student Athlete Protection Act of 1983," sponsored by Sen. Arlen Specter, R-Pa., would provide an antitrust exemption for professional sports leagues that barred recruitment of college players with remaining eligibility. However, many observers doubt that the bill, which has been criticized as special interest legislation, will become law. Specter himself noted that, "Given the limited timespan of a professional football career and the possibility of a collegiate injury precluding a later professional career, there is some validity to the contention that college players should be free to seek lucrative contracts before finishing their education and eligibility."

Many coaches contend that any loosening of eligibility standards would result in a ruinous defection of college football players to the pros. But the experience of the National Basketball Association appears to belie these fears. In the 12 years since the NBA opened its ranks to undergraduates, only 101 players have left college to turn professional. They include some of the game's biggest stars, such as Earvin "Magic" Johnson, who joined the Los Angeles Lakers in 1979 after his sophomore year at Michigan State University, and James Worthy, who joined the Lakers in 1982 after his junior year at the University of North Carolina. But other players, including four-time All-American center Ralph Sampson of the University of Virginia, have rejected multimillion-dollar offers to remain in college and pursue their degrees.

Concern About Athletes' Academic Records

The fear that many student athletes are leaving school with neither an education nor prospects for a professional sports career was on the minds of many of those who criticized Herschel Walker's decision to turn pro. They point out that of the 101 players who left college early to join the NBA, 25 were never even drafted, and 19 played one year or less. But others believe these professions of concern are hypocritical. A study conducted for the National Football League Players Association (NFLPA) in 1980 found that only 34 percent of NFL players, all of whom had exhausted their college eligibility, had actually received college degrees.[8] NFLPA President Ed Garvey told a March 17 Senate Judiciary Committee hearing on the Specter bill that

---

[8] The NFLPA is the players' union. The report, entitled "Institutional Discrimination," was written by Jomills Henry Braddock II of The Johns Hopkins University in Baltimore.

eligibility, not education, was the main concern of college coaches.

Of course, not all schools run "sports factories" that are only concerned with keeping athletes healthy enough to play. Notre Dame University, which has one of the oldest football traditions in the country, won the 1982 College Football Association Academic Achievement Award, because 84 percent of the financially aided football players who entered the school in 1976 had received their degrees within five years. The University of North Carolina claims that of the 128 athletes who played for basketball coach Dean Smith over 21 seasons through 1982, 121 graduated.

But at many schools, student athletes have been allowed to slide through classes, earning just enough credits to meet athletic eligibility standards. Before 1981, the only NCAA academic standard for athletic eligibility was that a student had to be making satisfactory progress toward a degree as defined by the institution. In 1981, a new rule was instituted that required athletes to average 12 semester or quarter hours for each term of enrollment, or 24 semester or 36 quarter hours since the beginning of the student's last season of competition. Not until this year was there a requirement that the credits be applicable to a specific degree.

Some of the biggest college athletic scandals of recent years have dealt with the doctoring of grade transcripts and the use of credits from phony correspondence courses to bolster athletes' academic records. For example, the University of New Mexico basketball program was found guilty of a number of violations in 1980, including admitting an athlete "on the basis of a counterfeit transcript from a community college," and arranging for an athlete to receive eight summer school credits "with full knowledge that the young man would not be required to attend class sessions or perform required class assignments."

Occasionally, there is a well-publicized story about an athlete who has completed his athletic eligibility but received no education at all. Kevin Ross, 23-year-old basketball star at Creighton University in Omaha, Neb., completed his athletic eligibility last year, then enrolled in the seventh grade at West Side Preparatory School in Chicago to learn how to read and write. "It doesn't mean anything that you have 20 Nobel Prize winners on your campus if you graduate people who simply cannot read," said Bob Aaron of the American Council on Education.

New NCAA Rules on Academic Requirements

The council was involved in drafting the new academic requirements for athletes adopted by the NCAA at their 77th annual convention, held in San Diego on Jan. 10-12, 1983. One measure, known as Rule 48, will require incoming freshman athletes at the NCAA's 277 Division I schools[9] to have at least a 2.0 high school grade-point average (out of 4.0) in a core curriculum of 11 academic courses, including English, history, math and science.[10] They will also be required to score a minimum 700 points (out of a possible 1,600 points) on the Scholastic Aptitude Test (SAT) or a minimum of 15 points (of a possible 35) on the American Collegiate Testing (ACT) exam. Rule 48 is scheduled to take effect in August 1986. The other proposal, known as Rule 56, will take effect in August 1984. It will require athletes in Division I schools to be enrolled in and pursuing credits toward specific degree programs.

"It doesn't mean anything that you have 20 Nobel Prize winners on your campus if you graduate people who simply cannot read."

Bob Aaron, public affairs
director, American Council
on Education

Both rules were meant to address the charge that schools often neglect the academic performances of athletes. It is not uncommon for young athletes to be given "special treatment" by teachers, often at the behest of coaches. "Some high school teachers, when they know a kid has a chance for a college scholarship, might help the kid out," said Gothard Lane, director of non-revenue sports at the University of Maryland, who added that many athletes are conned into believing that athletic success is all they will need to prepare for the future.

The problem is particularly severe in black ghettoes, where the main role models for many youngsters are the highly paid athletes they see on television. Much of the impetus for raising athletes' academic requirements came from black activists such as Harry Edwards, sociology professor at the University of California at Berkeley. Edwards has long complained that the

---

[9] NCAA schools are divided into three divisions. Division I includes the schools with the largest, most competitive athletic programs. It is split into two subdivisions: Division I-A, for schools with the largest football programs, and Division I-AA, for schools that have more modest athletic budgets or that have de-emphasized football in order to concentrate on basketball. Division II schools usually have smaller budgets and provide fewer athletic scholarships than Division I schools. Division III schools are the least competitive; many provide no athletic scholarships.

[10] Under the rules, the athletes would have to take at least three years of high school English, two years of mathematics, two years of social science and two years of natural or physical science.

educational/athletic system exploits black youths for their athletic talent, then discards them when their usefulness has ended. At a 1981 forum on college sports, Edwards described how this process of exploitation begins:

"As soon as someone finds that one kid in grammar school can run a little bit faster, hit a little bit harder, throw a ball a little bit farther than all of his or her peers, he or she becomes . . . 'something special,' [Edwards said]. And by the time this individual gets to high school . . . so little has been demanded of him academically that he has come to expect virtually nothing of himself academically." [11]

Despite wide support for ending such exploitation, many black groups have attacked Rule 48, particularly the requirement that entering freshman athletes achieve minimum scores on standardized tests. They argue that standardized tests are culturally biased in favor of white Americans and that this explains why a disproportionate number of black students do poorly on them. For example, black students taking the 1982 SAT test had an average combined score of 707, while white students scored an average of 927.

Some black groups claim that the white sports establishment is using the guise of improving academic performance as a "racist" tool to exclude black athletes. Other black groups take a softer line in opposing the standardized test requirement. Alan Kirschner, research director for the United Negro College Fund, said his organization "does not feel that the tests themselves are racially biased." But he also pointed out that no academic institution uses standardized test scores as the sole criteria for admission. Many other factors, such as grade-point average, motivation, and leadership potential, are taken into account. The College Board and its Educational Testing Service agree on this point. "Test scores should never be used alone in determining admission to college," said College Board President George Hanford. "The NCAA's action violates that principle by establishing a minimum 700 combined SAT score as a *necessary* . . . requirement for freshman athletic eligibility." [12]

Proponents of Rule 48 say that the use of a standardized test score is needed because a grade-point average may not be an accurate reflection of academic achievement. "It's a recognition that there is much academic unevenness in America's high schools," said Bob Aaron of the American Council on Educa-

---

[11] The forum was held Sept. 10-11, 1981, at the Center for the Study of Democratic Institutions at the University of California at Santa Barbara.

[12] Hanford made the statement in a speech before the Conference on Sport and Higher Education at Skidmore College, Saratoga Springs, N.Y. on March 18, 1983. Hanford also strongly denied that SAT tests are racially or culturally biased. For background, see "College Admissions," *E.R.R.*, 1980 Vol. I, pp. 265-284.

Player Agents

The involvement of lawyer Jack Manton in the Herschel Walker signing revived the controversy over player agents and college athletes. The Walker case was not the first in which an agent had a controversial role. In 1980, Jeff Ruland, now a star with the NBA's Washington Bullets, lost his last year of eligibility at Iona College in New Rochelle, N.Y., after entering into a agreement with and accepting cash from an agent. In 1971, Villanova University's surprise second-place finish in the NCAA basketball tournament was voided after star Howard Porter admitted having signed a professional contract through an agent earlier in the season.

In interviews with Editorial Research Reports, representatives of college coaches, the NCAA and the USFL all said that college sports were in danger of being overrun by "unscrupulous agents." According to Charles McClendon of the American Football Coaches Association, "It's a worse problem than people would imagine." David Berst, NCAA enforcement director, expressed stronger sentiments: "I would give you a scathing opinion of at least 98 percent of the agents. Agents do not work on behalf of the student athletes, they work on behalf of making money for themselves."

Some sports observers say the role of "unscrupulous" agents would be reduced if the schools made more of an effort to inform and counsel athletes. McClendon insisted that this would be one of the beneficial effects of the Walker case. "You're going to see better counseling," said McClendon. "We've got the most qualified people in the world on our college campuses to help these people. It's kind of an obligation we have to them."

tion. Gothard Lane of the University of Maryland also believes standardized tests are less vulnerable to manipulation. "You can't have some coach go up to the Educational Testing Service and say, 'Hey, this kid's going to get a scholarship, can you give him 700,' " he said.

Rule 48 proponents also point out that the new rule will not prevent a school from admitting anyone who does not meet the standard or from giving that person an athletic scholarship; it will just prevent that person from participating in intercollegiate sports as a freshman. They say ineligibility will allow the student to meet standards without having to deal with the pressures of athletic competition, and will show confidence on the part of the school that the student can make it academically. But opponents say that most schools will simply not bother with athletes whose talents cannot be immediately utilized. "These [athletes] don't get contracts for full tuition out of the clear blue sky," said Herbert O. Reid, counsel to the National Association for Equal Opportunity in Higher Education (NAFEO). "It's because of their athletic ability and their ability to play now."

NAFEO officials, along with the Rev. Jesse Jackson, president of People United to Serve Humanity (PUSH), and other black leaders are considering a lawsuit to block Rule 48 if the NCAA does not modify it before it takes effect in 1986.

In contrast, the other rule adopted by the NCAA at its January convention caused little controversy. By forcing athletes to pursue a degree program, the NCAA hopes to end the practice in some schools of placing athletes in easy courses that do not improve their minds or their employability. "You can no longer major in eligibility," said Aaron. "You can't be taking basket weaving, you can't be taking the history of sports in America as a major curriculum."

Money and College Sports

COLLEGE COACHES are sensitive to charges that they neglect the educational welfare of their athletes. "The greatest bragging point any of us could have is for our players to graduate. That's one of our proud moments," Charles McClendon, executive director of the American Football Coaches Association and former head coach of Louisiana State University, said in a recent interview.

Nevertheless, cynics scoffed when coaches said that their players' educational well-being was at the bottom of their protests over the Herschel Walker incident. "What was all the fuss about?" sports editor Larry Eldridge wrote in *The Christian Science Monitor* on March 3. "Well, it's not about education, that's for sure.... It's about money, of course...." Star players like Herschel Walker can provide a school with a winning record, full stadiums, bowl game invitations, lucrative television appearances,[13] and millions of dollars for the school's athletic program.

Dr. Mitchell H. Raiborn, author of an NCAA report on the revenues and expenses of intercollegiate athletic programs, estimated that the 187 Division I schools with football programs

---

[13] The current contracts between ABC-TV and CBS-TV and the NCAA for the right to broadcast college football games during the 1982-83 and 1983-84 seasons reportedly total $263.4 million. Ironically, the University of Georgia, "victimized" in the Herschel Walker incident, has joined the University of Oklahoma in an antitrust suit filed last year in federal district court in Denver that seeks to free the schools from the NCAA contract, which limits their number of television appearances, so they can negotiate their own deals. On Sept. 14, 1982, U.S. District Court Judge Juan Burciaga in Oklahoma City voided the NCAA television contract, ruling that exclusive NCAA control of television rights violated the Sherman Antitrust Act. However, on Sept. 22, 1982, the ruling was stayed by the U.S. Court of Appeals for the 10th Circuit in Denver, pending an NCAA appeal. As of April 13, 1983, there had been no decision on the appeal.

spent a total of $606.44 million in 1981 on men's sports alone, an average of $3.24 million per school. Over 16 percent spent more than $5.6 million. Budgets for Division I schools with major basketball programs but no football teams averaged $631,000 in 1981. Running an athletic program is not even cheap for the least competitive institutions. Division III schools without football spent an average of $144,000 on men's sports in 1981.

These reported expenses include the costs of operating all sports, not just football and basketball. College athletic administrators say that the "big-money" label pinned on major college sports programs is unfair, since they help support the non-revenue sports that provide athletic opportunities to thousands of students. At Division I football schools, football and basketball programs provided 69 percent of all athletic program revenues in 1981; all other sports provided 4 percent. At other Division I schools, basketball alone provided 59 percent of the revenues, other sports 6 percent. "I get miffed when they say it's big business," said Gothard Lane of the University of Maryland. "The whole reason that it's a big business in football and basketball is because at Maryland we have 22 sports, and 20 don't make a dime."

The Cost of Upgrading Women's Athletics

The demands on college budgets have intensified since the passage of Title IX of the Educational Amendments of 1972, which states that "No person in the United States shall, on the basis of sex, be excluded from participation in, be denied the benefits of, or be subject to discrimination under any education program or activity receiving federal financial assistance." At the time Title IX passed, women's sports at most schools were drastically under-financed; some schools had no women's programs at all. Female athletes demanded greater opportunity; some feminists called for men's and women's sports to be funded equally, on a dollar-for-dollar basis.[14]

The male sports establishment reacted in horror; the NCAA filed suit, claiming that Title IX "may well signal the end of intercollegiate athletic programs as we have known them in recent decades." Opponents were unable to get the law overturned. But the argument that crippling revenue-producing football and basketball programs would debilitate all sports, including women's, was convincing. In 1975, the Department of Health, Education and Welfare drew up regulations to allow schools to fund women's programs on the basis of women's participation in varsity athletics. Since schools usually sponsor fewer teams for women than men, in sports that require fewer

---

[14] For background, see "Women in Sports," *E.R.R.*, 1977 Vol. I, pp. 329-348.

University of Maryland's women's basketball team vs. North Carolina State's team.

participants, the participation rate is lower and funding levels can therefore be restrained.

Nonetheless, most colleges and universities have worked within the spirit of the law by expanding their athletic programs for women. The number of women participating in intercollegiate athletics at NCAA schools more than doubled between 1971 and 1981, from 31,852 to 69,468. At Division I football schools, the average women's athletic budget increased from $161,000 in 1978 to $392,000 in 1981. At Division I schools without football, the average women's budget went up from $95,000 in 1978 to $188,000 in 1981. But women's sports were also big money losers: at the big football schools, expenses for women's sports outstripped revenues by better than 3-to-1.

Recruiting Violations and Other Problems

Revelations of illegal practices on the part of athletic officials or university representatives are not uncommon. Sometimes the violations deal with circumvention of educational eligibility standards. But more frequently, the violations involve gifts of cash, material objects or services to athletes. Many of the illegal activities occur during the recruiting process. Below are two

176

examples of recent recruiting violations, as reported by the NCAA:

Southern Methodist University: "During the 1978-79 academic year ... the head football coach led the prospect reasonably to believe that he would be able to sell his complimentary season football tickets for an amount substantially in excess of their face value."

Clemson University: "In January 1978, an assistant football coach offered inducements to a prospective student-athlete to attend the university that included substantial sums of cash ... a television set, a wardrobe and six complimentary football tickets for the university's home football contests."

Not all violations have to do with recruits. Some coaches will reward or placate varsity players by paying them "under-the-table." Along with its 1980 academic violations *(see p. 170)*, the University of New Mexico basketball team was found guilty by the NCAA of providing players and their families with cash, free transportation, hotel accommodations and telephone privileges.

However, college coaches and officials are not always to blame for violations of NCAA rules. Overzealous alumni or "boosters" who commit illegal acts in the name of a school, even if they are acting independently of the coaches and administration, are regarded by the NCAA as "representatives of the university." "The most difficult factor for us to deal with runs to the attitude of the boosters and alumni of particular institutions," said David Berst, NCAA director of enforcement. "If they have a mindset that cheating is the way to succeed, then regardless of the intentions of the president of the institution, there will be much difficulty in trying to control the program."

The NCAA, which had only two enforcement officers a decade ago, has expanded the staff to 10 full-time and 25 part-time investigators. Berst estimated that 15 percent of all NCAA schools are involved in illegal activities at any given time. Ed Garvey of the NFLPA said he was certain that there were more violations than were reported, adding, "If a coach's job depends on getting the talent into his school ... the temptations are tremendous. Human nature is such that somebody's going to cheat on the rules."

Push for System's Reform

DEMANDS to "clean up" college sports are hardly new. Reform movements date back to the turn of the century, when concern centered on brutality in college football. Dangerous formations such as the "flying wedge" — in which blockers locked arms to guard the ball carrier and stampeded anyone who got in their way — resulted in hundreds of crippling injuries and dozens of deaths. A threat by President Theodore Roosevelt to ban football if the situation was not remedied resulted in the formation of the NCAA in 1906 and the establishment of most of the rules familiar to football fans today.

College football subsequently enjoyed a burst of popularity. Attending games became an "in" thing for Ivy League alumni, and the only thing to do in the small, entertainment-starved Midwestern towns that housed land-grant state universities. But with popularity came controversy, especially after schools began to openly recruit outstanding athletes for their teams. Scholarships based on athletic rather than academic ability, then considered unethical by many academicians, became common. So were "tramp athletes" or "ringers," thinly disguised professionals who often played for more than one school.[15]

In 1929, the Carnegie Foundation for the Advancement of Education, in a report entitled "American College Athletics," declared that "college sports have been developed from games played by boys for pleasure into systematic professionalized athletic contests." The foundation's protest against the commercialization of college sports sounds familiar:

"The paid coach, the gate receipts, the special training tables, the costly sweaters and extensive journeys . . . the recruiting from high school, the demoralizing publicity showered on the players, the devotion of an undue proportion of time to training, the devices for putting a desirable athlete, but a weak scholar, across the hurdles of the examinations — these ought to stop and the intercollege and intramural sports be brought back to a stage in which they can be enjoyed by large numbers of students and where they do not involve an expenditure of time and money wholly at variance with any ideal of honest study."

Some schools took the Carnegie report to heart. The University of Chicago, where the legendary Amos Alonzo Stagg had coached for 41 years,[16] determined in 1939 that big-time football conflicted with its academic traditions. When he announced that the school was dropping football, school President Robert Maynard Hutchins said, "To be successful, you must cheat. Everyone is cheating, and I refuse to cheat." Dozens of other schools, most of them private colleges, either dropped or de-emphasized varsity athletics, either because of the moral issues

---

[15] The Marx Brothers parodied such irregularities in their 1932 movie, "Horsefeathers."
[16] Stagg set a record for career victories (314) in his 58 years as a head coach (1889-1946) that was broken only in 1981 by Paul "Bear" Bryant of the University of Alabama. Bryant, who died in January 1983 shortly after his retirement, won 323 games in 25 years.

involved or because they could not afford to compete against the burgeoning state-funded public institutions.

But overall, college athletics got bigger, not smaller. The growth of college basketball that began in the 1930s was barely hindered by gambling scandals in the early 1950s and 1960s,[17] and television money helped college football weather the growth of pro football. Football gate receipts and television revenue enabled schools to promote many intramural and club-level sports to varsity level.

But the turbulence of the 1960s caused many cultural institutions, including college athletics, to be questioned. Scholars again questioned the propriety of sports as entertainment in the intellectual environment of the university. Student activists accused "jocks" of being tools of the establishment. Black athletes accused college administrators of exploitation, and women athletes demanded equal rights. A report written by George Hanford for the American Council on Education in 1974 called for the creation of a national commission to study the long-standing problems of college athletics.[18]

The momentum for reform has increased in recent years. A committee of college presidents was formed by the American Council on Education in July 1982 to study such issues as academic standards, recruitment and enforcement, governance of the NCAA, divisional structure of the NCAA, and the role of television in college sports. It was this committee that drafted the resolutions on raising academic requirements for athletes that were adopted at the NCAA convention in January *(see p. 170)*.

Suggestions That College Sports Turn Pro

Like the authors of the Carnegie Foundation report more than a half-century ago, some academicians believe that big-time college sports should be eliminated, not reformed. Maurice Mitchell, former chancellor of the University of Denver, has called intercollegiate athletics "an evil and a sin." "The only justification for anything that happens at a university is that it has educational value," he added. But college sports have become integral features on many campuses. "College sports are deeply embedded in higher education, and we simply waste our time if we think there is any way that they can be extracted

---

[17] In 1945, five Brooklyn College basketball players were expelled after accepting bribes to throw a game. In 1951, 33 players at seven New York City schools, including 1950 national champion City College of New York, were indicted for "fixing" games; two spent time in prison. In 1961, 37 players at 22 schools were accused of game-fixing. In 1981, former Boston College player Rick Kuhn was sentenced to 10 years in prison for his role in a gambling racket.

[18] Hanford et al., "A Report to the American Council on Education on the Need for a National Study of Intercollegiate Athletics," 1974.

from the fabric of American higher education in the next 10 or 20 years," said Harold Enarson, former president of Ohio State University.[19]

Some observers have suggested turning teams at the major sports schools into bona fide professional enterprises, operated independently of the school administration. In his 1980 book *The Recruiting Game*, John Rooney wrote: "Separate the athletic function, the revenue sports, from the traditional form of university control and allow a select group of collegiate football and basketball teams to become second-order, or minor league ... professional franchises located in the university community." Rooney suggested that players be allowed to play for up to five years, with salaries escalating to a maximum of $20,000. Players who wanted to take advantage of the educational facilities of the university could do so. Non-revenue sports would return to the original philosophy of participation for its own sake.

Others say that intercollegiate competition is already a professional enterprise. Ed Garvey of the NFLPA called on colleges to pay athletes the minimum wage, provide them with workers' compensation if they are disabled, and guarantee their scholarships until they get their degrees, regardless of how long it takes. But in a recent poll conducted for *The Chronicle of Higher Education*, 82 percent of the college presidents interviewed said they opposed turning big-time athletics into professional programs.[20] Many of the black leaders who accuse college sports of being exploitative also have little interest in professionalizing the games. "We are not interested in the perpetuation of the business and commercial activity of sports on college campuses," said Herbert O. Reid. "We want to protect the victims of that in making sure they get an education."

Drafting of an 'Athlete's Bill of Rights'

Black activists, including the Rev. Jesse Jackson and sociologist Harry Edwards, are drafting an "Athlete's Bill of Rights," which they believe should be part of the athletes' "contract" with the university. One proposal is that athletes' scholarships be guaranteed for five years. Many believe it is nearly impossible for athletes to handle their athletic obligations and keep up with their studies. They contend that athletes should be allowed to carry lighter course loads during their periods of eligibility while spreading their education over longer periods of time.

---

[19] Mitchell and Enarson were speaking at the 1981 forum on college sports at the Center for the Study of Democratic Institutions at the University of California, Santa Barbara.

[20] John A. Crowl, "NCAA Can Prevent Abuses, Many College Chiefs Say," *The Chronicle of Higher Education*, Jan. 5, 1983.

The Ivy League Model

The "Ivy League" schools — Brown, Columbia, Cornell, Dartmouth, Harvard, Pennsylvania, Princeton and Yale — long complemented their outstanding academic reputations with athletic prowess. A crew race between Yale and Harvard in 1852 is regarded as the first intercollegiate athletic contest. In 1869, Princeton played Rutgers in what is believed to be the first college football game, and the Ivies remained dominant on the gridiron through the "raccoon coat" era of college football.

However, by the early 1950s, the presidents of the Ivy League's big three — Harvard, Yale and Princeton — determined that growing costs and commercialization made academic integrity and big-time college sports incompatible. On Oct. 28, 1951, these schools voted to de-emphasize athletics; the other Ivy League schools soon followed. Scholarships based on athletic ability alone were banned, as were out-of-season practices.

Proponents of the Ivy League philosophy say that it is more beneficial for the student athlete. According to Columbia's athletic director, Alvin Paul, "It's important to make sure that the young men on the teams have a good experience and enjoy playing, because there are no athletic scholarships and the young men play because they want to play." Paul said that Columbia's coaches are judged not only on their won-loss records, as they are at other schools, but on the attrition rate of the players, which is regarded as an indication of how well the players are enjoying the experience.

College sports fans tend to ignore the Ivy League. It has been decades since an Ivy football team was nationally competitive. But league teams still pull some surprises; Princeton's basketball team won two games before being eliminated from the recent NCAA tournament. And some outstanding athletes have attended the Ivy schools since sports started being de-emphasized, including Princeton's Bill Bradley, now a U.S. senator from New Jersey and a former basketball star for the championship New York Knicks team.

Paul said there is far less pressure from alumni than there is at a big-time sports school. He admitted that there are a few alumni who played on Columbia's 1934 Rose Bowl team who wish for a return of the good old days, but added that "the vast majority understand the Ivy League philosophy and why the youngsters are here in the first place."

Other proposals in the "Bill of Rights" include improved tutoring and counseling services for athletes and disclosure by schools to potential recruits of the percentage of their athletes who have received degrees. But the proposal that has the greatest support in the academic community is one that would make all freshmen ineligible for athletic competition. Freshmen were ineligible until the 1972-73 season when the NCAA rule was lifted, mainly because of the high cost of running "junior varsity" programs for the ineligible players.

181

Many observers see the pressures of athletic competition as an unfair burden on freshman athletes, most of whom are living away from home for the first time. These athletes are given little opportunity to acclimate themselves to the academic environment: at some schools, freshmen play in as many as three football games before they attend their first classes. These time demands were cited by supporters of the new NCAA rules as the rationale for barring marginal students from athletic competition.

"The key to controlling intercollegiate athletic programs rests with the president of the institution. That is the only individual who has the clout to control the staff members who work under him...."

David Berst, director of enforcement,
National Collegiate Athletic Association

Many black groups that oppose Rule 48 on the ground that it is discriminatory agree, however, that athletic competition is too demanding for freshmen and would support a universal freshman ineligibility rule. "If it was uniform, absolutely," said Alan Kirschner of the United Negro College Fund. College administrators are also becoming more favorable to the idea. "You don't have to be a soothsayer to know that this is the direction that these college presidents are going in," said Bob Aaron of the American Council on Education. But college athletic officials say that, in order to maintain their pools of available talent, they would need to provide more grants-in-aid, running up the already high costs of intercollegiate competition.

Creating a New Balance in College Sports

Additional expense is one thing that many schools, especially those with less successful programs, can ill afford. Because of its high costs and low revenues, Villanova University's once-powerful football program was dropped in 1980 so the school could concentrate on its successful and popular basketball program. The University of Nevada-Las Vegas, another school with a lucrative basketball program, announced in January that it was cutting $400,000 from its football program, which lost $600,000 last year. Wagner College in Staten Island, N.Y., which only a few years ago appeared on the verge of developing a competitive basketball program, announced in March that it would move its athletic program from Division I to the less competitive Division II, and eventually to Division III.

Other schools have de-emphasized sports to protect their reputations and academic integrity. The University of San Francisco (USF) basketball team was a traditional power, producing such stars as all-time NBA great Bill Russell of the Boston Celtics. But the program was also in constant trouble; the NCAA placed the team on probation in 1978 and 1980. Finally, in 1982, after star player Quentin Dailey was convicted of aggravated assault and evidence of illegal payments to athletes was revealed, the school's president, the Rev. John Lo Schiavo, announced that the basketball program would be eliminated.

The recent interest shown by college presidents in the conduct of their athletic programs is seen as a sign that college sports can be cleaned up. "The key to controlling intercollegiate athletic programs rests with the president of the institution," said David Berst of the NCAA. "That is the only individual who has the clout to control the staff members who work under him, or who has the kind of rapport and clout with boosters and alumni to encourage a course of action on behalf of the institution."

The current reform movement is seen by some observers as a turning point for college athletics. Such claims have been heard before. In his 1974 report for the American Council on Education, George Hanford wrote that "college sports are at a crossroads." But it took almost a full decade for college officials to act on some of the problems outlined in the report. It remains to be seen if college sports are into a sustained period of reform, or if this is just another inning in a long, low-scoring contest.

Selected Bibliography

Books

Durso, Joseph et al., *The Sports Factory*, Quadrangle, 1975.
Michener, James A., *Sports in America*, Random House, 1976.
Rooney, John F. Jr., *The Recruiting Game: Toward A New System of Intercollegiate Athletics*, University of Nebraska Press, 1980.

Articles

Boyle, Robert H. and Roger Jackson, "Bringing Down The Curtain," *Sports Illustrated*, Aug. 9, 1982.
"College Sports in Trouble," *The Center Magazine*, January-February 1982.
Hill, Henry and Douglas S. Looney, "How I Put The Fix In," *Sports Illustrated*, Feb. 16, 1981.
Hogan, Candace Lyle, "Revolutionizing School and Sports: 10 Years of Title IX," *Ms.*, May 1982.
Telander, Rick, "The Descent of a Man," *Sports Illustrated*, March 8, 1982.
Underwood, John, "Does Herschel Have Georgia On His Mind?" *Sports Illustrated*, March 1, 1982.
Zimmerman, Paul, "A New Round of Star Wars?" *Sports Illustrated*, March 7, 1983.

Reports and Studies

Atwell, Robert H., "The Money Game: Financing Collegiate Athletics," American Council on Education, 1980.
Braddock, Jomills Henry II, "Institutional Discrimination: A Study of Managerial Recruitment in Professional Football," National Football League Players Association, September 1980.
Editorial Research Reports: "Women in Sports," 1977 Vol. I, p. 329; "Future of Varsity Sports," 1975 Vol. II, p. 645.
Hanford, George H., "A Report to the American Council on Education on the Need for a National Study of Intercollegiate Athletics," 1974.
Raiborn, Mitchell H., "Revenues and Expenses of Intercollegiate Athletic Programs, 1978-1981," National Collegiate Athletic Association, 1982.

Cover illustration by Staff Artist Robert Redding; photo p. 168 courtesy of the New Jersey Generals; photo p. 176 courtesy of the University of Maryland.

INDEX